AAT

GW00504647

Level 2

Certificate in Accounting

Synoptic Assessment

Exam Practice Kit

For assessments from
September 2024

Eighteenth edition 2024

ISBN: 9781 0355 1646 9

Previous ISBN: 9781 0355 0688 0

e-ISBN: 9781 0355 1681 0

British Library Cataloguing-in-Publication Data

A catalogue record for this book is available from the British Library

Published by

BPP Learning Media Ltd

BPP House, Aldine Place

142–144 Uxbridge Road

London W12 8AA

learningmedia.bpp.com

Printed in the United Kingdom

Your learning materials, published by BPP Learning Media Ltd, are printed on paper obtained from traceable sustainable sources.

A note about copyright

Contents

Introduction

This is BPP Learning Media's AAT Exam Practice Kit for the *Certificate in Accounting Level 2 Synoptic Assessment*. It is part of a suite of ground-breaking resources produced by BPP Learning Media for AAT assessments.

This Exam Practice Kit has been carefully designed to enable students to practise all of the learning outcomes and assessment criteria for the units that make up the *Certificate in Accounting Level 2 Synoptic Assessment*. It is fully up to date as at April 2024 and reflects both the AAT's qualification specification and the sample assessment provided by the AAT.

This Exam Practice Kit contains these key features:

- Tasks corresponding to each assessment objective in the qualification specification and related task in the synoptic assessment. Some tasks in this Exam Practice Kit are designed for learning purposes, others are of assessment standard.

The emphasis in all tasks and assessments is on the practical application of the skills acquired.

VAT

You may find tasks throughout this Exam Practice Kit that need you to calculate or be aware of a rate of VAT. This is stated at 20% in these examples and questions.

Test specification

Assessment method	Marking type	Duration of assessment
Computer-based synoptic assessment	Partially computer/partially human marked	2 hours

Synoptic assessment objectives		Weighting
Assessment objective 1 Related learning outcomes:	Demonstrate an understanding of the different business types and their functions The Business Environment LO4 Understand the impact of setting up different types of business entity LO5 Understand the finance function within an organisation	10%
Assessment objective 2 Related learning outcomes:	Demonstrate an understanding of the finance function, its information requirements and sources, and its role in the wider organisation The Business Environment LO5 Understand the finance function within an organisation LO6 Produce work in appropriate formats and communicate effectively LO7 Understand the importance of information to business operations	13%

Synoptic assessment objectives		Weighting
Assessment objective 3 Related learning outcomes:	Demonstrate an understanding of corporate social responsibility (CSR), ethics and sustainability The Business Environment LO3 Understand the principles of corporate social responsibility (CSR), ethics and sustainability	14%
Assessment objective 4 Related learning outcomes:	Process bookkeeping transactions and communicate information Introduction to Bookkeeping LO1 Understand how to set up bookkeeping systems LO2 Process customer transactions LO3 Process supplier transactions The Business Environment LO6 Produce work in appropriate formats and communicate effectively	22%
Assessment objective 5 Related learning outcomes:	Produce and reconcile control accounts, and use journals to correct errors Principles of Bookkeeping Controls LO1 Use control accounts LO2 Reconcile a bank statement with the cash book LO3 Use the journal	10%
Assessment objective 6 Related learning outcomes:	Demonstrate an understanding of the principles of contract law The Business Environment LO1 Understand the principles of contract law	7%
Assessment objective 7 Related learning outcomes:	Demonstrate an understanding of bookkeeping systems, receipts and payments, and the importance of information and data security The Business Environment LO7 Understand the importance of information to business operations Introduction to Bookkeeping LO1 Understand how to set up bookkeeping systems LO2 Process customer transactions LO3 Process supplier transactions **Principles of Bookkeeping Controls** LO1 Use control accounts LO2 Reconcile a bank statement with the cash book LO3 Use the journal	10%

Synoptic assessment objectives		Weighting
Assessment objective 8 Related learning outcomes:	Demonstrate an understanding of the global business environment The Business Environment LO2 Understand the external business environment	14%
Total		100%

Approaching the assessment

When you sit the assessment it is very important that you follow the on screen instructions. This means you need to carefully read the instructions, both on the introduction screens and during specific tasks.

When you access the assessment you should be presented with an introductory screen with information similar to that shown below

---

Assessment information:

Instructions

- Read the scenario carefully before attempting the questions, you can return to it at any time by clicking on the 'Introduction' button at the bottom of the screen.
- **Complete all 8 tasks.**
- Answer the questions in the spaces provided. For answers requiring free text entry, the box will expand to fit your answer.
- Tasks may require extended writing as part of your response to the question. You should make sure you allow adequate time to complete these tasks.
- You must use a full stop to indicate a decimal point. For example, write 100.57 not 100,57 or 100 57
- Both minus signs and brackets can be used to indicate negative numbers unless task instructions say otherwise.
- You may use a comma to indicate a number in the thousands, but you don't have to.
- For example, 10000 and 10,000 are both acceptable.
- Where the date is relevant, it is given in the task data.

Information

- The total time for this paper is **2 hours**.
- The total mark for this paper is 100.
- The marks for each sub-task are shown alongside the task.

The actual instructions will vary depending on the subject you are studying for. It is very important you read the instructions on the introductory screen and apply them in the assessment. You don't want to lose marks when you know the correct answer just because you have not entered it in the right format.

In general, the rules set out in the AAT practice assessments for the subject you are studying for will apply in the real assessment, but you should carefully read the information on this screen again in the real assessment, just to make sure. This screen may also confirm the VAT rate used if applicable.

A full stop is needed to indicate a decimal point. We would recommend using minus signs to indicate negative numbers and leaving out the comma signs to indicate thousands, as this results in a lower number of keystrokes and less margin for error when working under time pressure.

Having said that, you can use whatever is easiest for you as long as you operate within the rules set out for your particular assessment.

You have to show competence throughout the assessment, and you should therefore complete all of the tasks. Don't leave questions unanswered.

In some assessments, written or complex tasks may be human marked. In this case you are given a blank space or table to enter your answer into. You are told in the assessments which tasks these are. Note there may be none if all answers are marked by the computer.

If these involve calculations, it is a good idea to decide in advance how you are going to lay out your answers to such tasks by practising answering them on a word document, and certainly you should try all such tasks in this Exam Practice Kit and in the AAT's environment using the practice assessment.

When asked to fill in tables, or gaps, never leave any blank even if you are unsure of the answer. Fill in your best estimate.

Note that for some assessments where there is a lot of scenario information or tables of data provided (eg tax tables), you may need to access these via 'pop-ups'. Instructions will be provided on how you can bring up the necessary data during the assessment.

Finally, take note of any task specific instructions once you are in the assessment. For example, you may be asked to enter a date in a certain format or to enter a number to a certain number of decimal places.

Grading

To achieve the qualification and to be awarded a grade, you must pass all the mandatory unit assessments, all optional unit assessments (where applicable) and the synoptic assessment.

The AAT Level 2 Certificate in Accounting will be awarded a grade. This grade will be based on performance across the qualification. Unit assessments are not individually graded. These assessments are given a mark that is used in calculating the overall grade.

How overall grade is determined

You will be awarded an overall qualification grade (Distinction, Merit, and Pass). If you do not achieve the qualification, you will not receive a qualification certificate, and the grade will be shown as unclassified.

The marks of each assessment will be converted into a percentage mark and rounded up or down to the nearest whole number. This percentage mark is then weighted according to the weighting of the unit assessment or synoptic assessment within the qualification. The resulting weighted assessment percentages are combined to arrive at a percentage mark for the whole qualification.

Grade definition	Percentage threshold
Distinction	90-100%
Merit	80-89%
Pass	70-79%
Unclassified	0-69% Or failure to pass one or more assessment/s

Re-sits

Some AAT qualifications such as the AAT Foundation Certificate in Accounting have restrictions in place for how many times you are able to re-sit assessments. Please refer to the AAT website for further details.

You should only be entered for an assessment when you are well prepared and you expect to pass the assessment.

 BPP

AAT qualifications

The material in this book may support the following AAT qualifications:

AAT Level 2 Certificate in Accounting and AAT Certificate in Accounting at SCQF Level 6.

Supplements

From time to time we may need to publish supplementary materials to one of our titles. This can be for a variety of reasons. From a small change in the AAT unit guidance to new legislation coming into effect between editions.

You should check our supplements page regularly for anything that may affect your learning materials. All supplements are available free of charge on our supplements page on our website at: learningmedia.bpp.com/pages/resources-for-students

Improving material and removing errors

BPP Learning Media does everything possible to ensure the material is accurate and up to date when sending to print. In the event that any errors are found after the print date, they are uploaded to the following website: learningmedia.bpp.com/pages/errata

Questions

Assessment objective 1 – The business environment

Task 1.1

(a) Identify whether the following statements about sole traders are true or false.

Statement	True ✓	False ✓
Sole traders do not have to share their profits with anyone.		
A sole trader has complete control over the business.		
Sole traders may employ staff.		

(b) Identify whether the following statements regarding entities and the entity concept are true or false.

Statement	True ✓	False ✓
Accounts of business entities reflect the financial position of the owners.		
The entity concept means that the owners of the business must be separate from those who manage it.		
Not all business entities have limited liability.		

(c) Identify whether the following statements regarding unlimited companies are true or false.

Statement	True ✓	False ✓
An unlimited company can be a private or public company.		
An unlimited company is not usually required to file a copy of its annual accounts and reports with the Registrar each year.		

Task 1.2

(a) Which function stores finished products before they are sold and distributes them to customers after their sale?

	✓
Logistics	
Operations	
Marketing	

 BPP

(b) Which function decides which products and services should be produced?

	✓
Marketing	
Finance	
Information technology	

(c) Which function obtains inputs and converts them into outputs?

	✓
Operations	
Information technology	
Logistics	

(d) Identify whether the following statements regarding entities and the entity concept are true or false.

Statement	True ✓	False ✓
An entity is a legal concept.		
The financial accounts of an entity should only reflect the entity's business activities and financial performance.		
An entity is a part of a business.		

(e) Identify whether the following statements regarding company names are true or false.

Statement	True ✓	False ✓
'Passing off' actions are used when a company takes another to court to dispute their use of a company name.		
Companies can complain about the use of a name by another company to the Registrar of Companies.		

Task 1.3

(a) A 'model' version of which of the following documents will be registered for a company if it is not supplied on registration.

	✓
Memorandum of association	
Articles of association	
Statement of compliance	

(b) Identify whether the following statements regarding the entity concept are true or false.

BPP

Statement	True ✓	False ✓
A company's shareholders jointly own the business's assets.		
A company must employ directors who are not the business's owners.		
A company is liable for its debts.		

(c) Which function involves checking the quality of products made?

	✓
Marketing	
Operations	
Human resources	

(d) Which function involves motivating employees?

	✓
Human resources	
Finance	
Logistics	

(e) Which function involves thinking about the future needs of customers?

	✓
Operations	
Marketing	
Finance	

Task 1.4

(a) Identify whether the following statements about partnerships are true or false.

Statement	True ✓	False ✓
Partners have the right to be involved in managing the partnership unless agreed otherwise.		
Partners are deemed to share profits equally unless agreed otherwise.		
Forming a limited liability partnership (LLP) is where the partners simply agree to run a business together.		

 BPP

(b) **Which function involves identifying new products and services and selling them to the customer?**

	✓
Human resources	
Logistics	
Sales and marketing	

(c) **Which function involves reporting to shareholders?**

	✓
Operations	
Finance	
Sales and marketing	

(d) **Which function involves ensuring the correct number of staff are employed?**

	✓
Finance	
Human resources	
Operations	

(e) **Finding a partner to perform a business process so that the business does not have to perform that process itself is known as:**

	✓
Upskilling	
Outsourcing	
Contracting out	

Task 1.5

(a) **Identify whether the followings statements about legal structures for businesses are true or false.**

Statement	True ✓	False ✓
Setting up a business as a company limited by guarantee means that business owners have to place money in a ring-fenced account which guarantees a sum of money is always available to pay the company's debts.		
A company can only raise money by selling shares if it is a public limited company.		
Close family are permitted to form partnerships if they wish.		

BPP

(b) Which of the following statements about 'off-the-shelf' companies is correct?

	✓
'Off-the-shelf' companies are usually formed with unique Articles of association.	
Purchasing an 'off-the-shelf' company means that the new owners do not have to file registration documents with the Registrar.	
Buying an 'off-the-shelf' company to avoid liability for pre-incorporation expenses does not work.	

(c) Which of the following is a tax that all limited liability companies must account for and pay?

	✓
Corporation tax	
VAT	
Inheritance tax	

Assessment objective 2 – The business environment

Task 2.1

It is Friday morning. A colleague usually banks the weekly cash on a Friday morning. As the colleague is on holiday, she has asked you to do it. Your line manager has also asked you to complete some project work which you think will take all of Friday. You are not sure you will have time to do both tasks and you know the business is suffering from cash flow problems.

Required

(a) Which TWO of the following are possible consequences of you NOT banking the money on Friday?

	✓
The business may have insufficient funds available to pay a debt becoming payable next week.	
You will not be able to complete the work for your line manager.	
You will be able to complete the work for your line manager.	
The money will not have to be banked by someone else.	

(b) Complete the following sentence.

The most appropriate action to take is:

Picklist

- Bank the money and then move on to the project work.
- Complete the project work and bank the money next week.
- Explain the situation to your manager and try to find a solution.
- Throw away the note from your colleague and claim you did not receive it.

Your weekly workload (excluding completed tasks) is shown in the table below. You need to carry out all these tasks, but you also have to respond to business needs as required. Your working day is 9:30am to 5:30pm. Your lunch break is an hour long (12:30pm to 1:30pm). It is 9:30am on Wednesday and you have completed your routine tasks on time so far this week.

Your remaining tasks for the week are as follows:

Task	Task to be completed by:		Task duration
	Day	Time	
Receivables reconciliation	Thursday	09:30	45 minutes
Supplier statement reconciliations	Thursday	10:15	1 hour
Calculate depreciation and process the related journals	Wednesday	11:30	1.5 hours
Collect and distribute post	Every day	10:00	30 minutes
Enter cash payments and receipts	Every day	17:00	3 hours
Prepare payroll listing	Friday	15:00	1 hour
Bank reconciliation	Friday	13:00	2 hours

On arriving at your desk, you pick up an email informing you that the managing director has called a meeting to brief all employees on a proposed project to relocate the business to another nearby premises. All employees must attend the briefing at 11:30am which will last for 1 hour.

Required

(c) **Complete the to-do list below for Wednesday by selecting the appropriate tasks from the picklist provided.**

Wednesday To-do list		Order of task completion
	▼	First task
	▼	Second task
	▼	Third task
	▼	Fourth task
	▼	Fifth task
	▼	Sixth task

Picklist

- Bank reconciliation
- Briefing from managing director
- Calculate depreciation and process the related journals
- Collect and distribute post
- Enter cash payments and receipts
- Prepare payroll listing
- Receivables reconciliation
- Supplier statement reconciliations

Task 2.2

You are a trainee in the accounting function, and you work for both the financial accounting and management accounting functions. You work from 9:00am until 5:00pm and are required to have lunch between 12:00pm and 1:00pm.

The following tables show your work schedules for the financial and management accounting functions and detail the days when specific jobs have to be completed and the length of time, in hours, each job takes you to complete. The financial accounting function works on a monthly cycle of work whereas the management accounting function works on a weekly cycle of work. For the financial accounting function, work is required by the end of the day identified in the work schedule.

Financial accounting function work schedule					
	Monday	**Tuesday**	**Wednesday**	**Thursday**	**Friday**
Week 1	Bank reconciliation (2 hours)			Bank monies (2 hours)	Trade receivables review (3 hours)
Week 2		Petty cash top up (2 hours)	Supplier payments (3 hours)	Bank monies (2 hours)	

Financial accounting function work schedule					
	Monday	**Tuesday**	**Wednesday**	**Thursday**	**Friday**
Week 3	Bank reconciliation (2 hours)	Accruals and prepayments (2 hours)		Bank monies (2 hours)	Trade receivables review (3 hours)
Week 4	Wages analysis (3 hours)		Non-current assets (1 hour)	Bank monies (2 hours)	

Management accounting function work schedule			
Task	**Task to be completed by:**		**Task duration**
	Day	**Time**	
Budget run	Friday	09:00	4 hours
Expenses analysis	Tuesday	14:00	2 hours
Departmental reports	Monday	12:00	2 hours
Inventory review	Friday	10:00	1 hour
Variance report	Every day	14:00	1 hour
Departmental charges	Wednesday	12:00	2 hours

In addition to this information, the whole accounting function has an hour-long meeting at 10:00am on Mondays. Today is Friday in week three of the month.

Required

Complete the to-do list below for next Monday by assigning each task to the correct position using the picklist.

Please note that each task box is one hour in duration therefore, if a task takes more than one hour to complete, you will be able to use the task box more than once.

Monday To-do list	Time
▼	09:00–10:00
▼	10:00–11:00
▼	11:00–12:00
▼	12:00–13:00
▼	13:00–14:00
▼	14:00–15:00
▼	15:00–16:00
▼	16:00–17:00

Picklist

- Accounting function meeting

- Accruals and prepayments
- Bank monies
- Bank reconciliation
- Budget run
- Departmental charges
- Departmental reports
- Expenses analysis
- Inventory review
- Lunch
- Non-current assets
- Petty cash top up
- Supplier payments
- Trade receivables review
- Variance report
- Wages analysis

Task 2.3

(a) Which ONE of the following policies and procedures is most likely to be relevant to those working in an accounting function?

	✓
Production quality control policy	
Website development procedures	
Staff code of behaviour policy	
Motor vehicle maintenance policy	

(b) Identify which TWO of the following statements are correct.

	✓
Organisations, by law, must have at least ten policies and procedures.	
It is good practice for organisations to have policies and procedures so all staff work to a consistent standard.	
Data protection policy is an example of a policy that would not apply to those staff working in an accounting function.	
Organisational procedures always result in staff taking longer to do work tasks.	
Ensuring staff adhere to organisational policies and procedures should result in more efficient working practices.	
The health and safety policy only applies to those working in the production department.	

You have been passed a company 'information' policy that your manager says is relevant to you when carrying out your daily tasks.

An extract from the policy is given below:

 BPP

- Information policy.
- Personal data must be accurate.
- Personal data must only be kept for as long as necessary.
- Personal data must be kept securely.
- No information about customers or employees must be revealed to other customers or employees.

Required

(c) **Complete the following sentence by selecting the appropriate option from the picklist.**

This policy has been compiled to aid compliance with [_____ ▼]

Picklist

- Confidentiality of information legislation.
- Data protection legislation.
- Employee protection legislation.
- The accounting department will provide information to other departments within the business.

Task 2.4

You have been asked to do an urgent task by your manager which means you will not be able to complete the work a senior colleague has already allocated to you to complete by the end of the day.

Required

(a) **Select the most appropriate action to take from the list provided in the table.**

	✓
Complete the additional task as your manager is the most senior person you work for, then do whatever other work you can. The colleague will have to wait for their work until you have time to complete it.	
Complete the additional task as your manager is the most senior person you work for, then do whatever other work you can. You will prioritise the colleague's work for the next day.	
Complete the colleague's work as they asked you to do the work first and you will start the manager's work tomorrow.	
Discuss your workload with both the manager and the colleague to decide on the work priority and renegotiate deadlines where appropriate.	

You have to check supplier statements on a Thursday so that your colleague can receive the necessary information for her to be able to pay appropriate suppliers. A critically important task has been left on your desk by your manager. If you complete this urgent task, you will not be able to check all the supplier statements and provide information to your colleague.

Required

(b) **Identify whether the following statements are true or false in relation to the impact on your colleague or the organisation if you do not supply the information on supplier statements.**

Statement	True ✓	False ✓
There will be no impact. If you cannot check supplier statements on Thursday, you can prioritise this work the next day.		
Your colleague may be unable to pay suppliers by the due date which may result in problems for the organisation in receiving future supplies.		

(c) **For each of the following actions, select what they primarily contribute to from the picklist.**

Action	Contributes to:
Reduce customer credit terms so they pay their debts earlier	▼
Ensure IT support is in place in case staff encounter computer problems	▼
Produce a health and safety policy to be circulated to all staff	▼
Ensure all staff are paid at least the minimum wage	▼
Ensure staff recruited for each job have the relevant experience and skills	▼
Avoid the build-up of surplus inventories	▼

Picklist

- Compliance with applicable laws and regulations
- The management of working capital and solvency
- The smooth running of the business

Task 2.5

As an accounts assistant, you work 9:00am to 5:00pm (with an hour for lunch at 1:00pm) and have the following routine duties (duration of tasks are in brackets):

- Open the morning post (30 minutes)
- Pass any cheques received to the cashier (30 minutes)
- Enter sales invoices/credit notes daily in batches into computer system by midday (2 hours)
- Match and check purchase invoices to goods received notes daily and pass them all to the accountant for authorisation (6 minutes per invoice) (see related information that follows on the deadline for this)
- File sales invoices/credit notes (between 1 and 2 hours of filing)

Today is Friday 27 September and having already opened the post and passed the cheques to the cashier, you get a telephone call from the accountant to say that one of your colleagues is not coming in today due to sickness. You now also need to enter the weekly purchase invoices into the computer (which should only take an hour). Another colleague, who is back in the office this afternoon (2:00pm), needs to review a list of these invoices before the end of the day for forecasting purposes. The list is generated from the computer system you are entering the invoices into.

You have 20 purchase invoices that need to be matched to (and checked against) GRNs before the end of the day, ready for authorisation first thing on Monday.

Required

(a) Decide on the order you would carry out the tasks included in the picklist.

Order	Task	
1st task		▼
2nd task		▼
3rd task		▼
4th task		▼

Picklist

- Enter sales invoices/credit notes into computer system
- Enter weekly purchase invoices into the computer
- Filing
- Match purchase invoices to goods received notes and pass to the accountant for authorisation

(b) Identify which TWO of the following actions will help the solvency of an organisation.

	✓
Maximise inventory levels	
Issue statements to trade receivables on a regular basis	
Pay trade payables as soon as invoices are received	
Encourage trade receivables to pay the amounts owed on or before the due date	
Ensure the organisation has a staff development policy	
Issue statements to trade payables on a regular basis	

Task 2.6

(a) Which of the following parties are responsible for a company's statutory financial statements?

	✓
The directors	
The shareholders	
The internal auditors	
The management accountants	

(b) Which of the following parties are responsible for a business' variance analysis?

	✓
The finance director	
The management accountants	
The external auditor	
The board of directors	

(c) Identify whether the following types of information are from internal or external sources.

Information	Internal ✓	External ✓
Employee salaries		
Tax rates		

(d) Identify whether the following statements about information are true or false.

Statement	True ✓	False ✓
An advantage of secondary information is that the investigator knows where the information has come from.		
A disadvantage of secondary information is that the investigator may not be aware of any inadequacies or limitations in the information.		

Task 2.7

(a) Which of the following parties is responsible for confirming a company's financial statements show a true and fair view?

	✓
The financial accountants	
The shareholders	
The external auditors	
The internal auditors	

(b) Which of the following parties is responsible for recording salary expenses in the accounts?

	✓
The financial accountants	
The management accountants	
The finance director	
The human resources function	

Required

(c) Identify which business function should receive the following information from the finance function.

Information supplied	Sales and marketing ✓	Logistics ✓
Details of inventory counts		
VAT rates on different products and services		
Credit notes issued to customers		

(d) Identify TWO principles of effective communication which should be followed by the finance function.

	✓
Concise	
Measurable	
Efficient	
Planned	
Compliant	
Complete	

Task 2.8

(a) Identify whether each of the policies below relate to a specific function or to the entire organisation.

Policy	Function-specific policy ✓	Organisation-wide policy ✓
Financial controls policy		
Equal opportunities policy		

(b) Match the type of accounts produced to the correct description.

Statement	Management accounts ✓	Statutory financial accounts ✓
Not regulated by law		
Filed with the Registrar of Companies		

You work in the finance department and have been told that a colleague has been sent home ill. The colleague was working on a report due to the finance director today (something only they do) and you have been asked to complete it.

Required

(c) How would you describe this task? Select all that apply.

	✓
Routine	
Urgent	
Unexpected	

Assessment objective 3 – The business environment

Task 3.1

(a) Identify whether the following statements are true or false.

Statement	True ✓	False ✓
Those working within an accounting environment do not need to act with integrity.		
Personal information of a client cannot be given to other people unless the client authorises it.		
Information about the income generated by a client listed on the stock exchange can be discussed with your friends as, at the end of the year, the organisation will publish its financial results.		
A conflict of interest never has to be declared if the employee feels happy about the situation.		

(b) Identify which TWO of the following are sustainability initiatives which a business may implement.

	✓
Hold all meetings face-to-face rather than virtually.	
Have all corridor, hall and passage lighting linked to motion sensors so they automatically switch off when no one is using them.	
Always select the most competitively priced suppliers of goods and services.	
Ensure all qualified accountants complete CPD.	
Do business with any organisations regardless of their environmental practices.	
Ensure costs and expenses are minimised in every instance.	
Arrange monthly management meetings virtually rather than at head office.	
Encourage employees to print out emails.	

(c) Write a short report for non-finance staff explaining:

    (1) What is meant by corporate social responsibility (CSR)

    (2) Some examples of good practice in CSR for an organisation

Task 3.2

(a) Using the picklist, identify THREE fundamental ethical principles.

Fundamental ethical principles	
	▼
	▼
	▼

Picklist

- Confidentiality
- Good communication
- Honesty
- Integration
- Integrity
- Objectivity
- Professionalism
- Subjectivity

(b) **Write a brief report for finance staff setting out:**

(1) **An introduction to the subject of ethical principles**

(2) **What is meant by professional behaviour**

(3) **Why confidentiality of information must be maintained**

(4) **Why these issues are particularly important in an accounts department**

Task 3.3

Organisations have a moral obligation to implement sustainability initiatives which promote the long-term maintenance and wellbeing of the environment, the economy and society as a whole.

Required

(a) **Identify which FOUR of the following are sustainability initiatives that a business may implement.**

	✓
Introduce a waste recycling scheme	
Recruit only fully trained staff	
Use video conferencing to save staff having to travel to team meetings	
Increase prices every time costs go up	
Obtain goods and services from the cheapest supplier	
Give all staff a pay rise every year	
Introduce procedures to ensure that all electrical equipment is fully switched off each day when the office is vacated	
Encourage staff not to print emails unless absolutely necessary	

(b) **Identify whether the following statements are true or false.**

Statement	True ✓	False ✓
Sustainability means ensuring the organisation focuses purely on economic growth at all costs.		
Encouraging suppliers to send electronic invoices can be part of an organisation's sustainability agenda.		

Statement	True ✓	False ✓
When sourcing goods and services, an organisation should check that potential suppliers have good environmental policies.		
Planning the routes of delivery vehicles to minimise distance travelled may reduce the running costs of the organisation and also have a positive effect on the environment.		

Task 3.4

(a) Identify which FOUR of the following are sustainability initiatives that a business may implement.

	✓
Arrange virtual rather than face-to-face team meetings	
Have all office lighting linked to motion sensors so they automatically switch off when the office is empty	
Always select the lowest priced suppliers of goods and services	
Ensure all trainee accountants complete CPD	
Do business only with organisations which can demonstrate they follow responsible environmental practices	
Ensure costs and expenses are minimised in every instance	
Arrange monthly management meetings at a central point in the country rather than at head office	
Restrict paper usage to the printing of essential documents only	

(b) Identify whether the following statements are true or false.

Statement	True ✓	False ✓
Sustainability means ensuring the organisation focuses purely on generating the highest profit irrespective of the consequences of the organisation's actions.		
When building new premises, trying to ensure the building is carbon neutral even if this results in increased initial costs is an example of a sustainable initiative by the organisation.		
Sustainable initiatives do not apply to those in an accounting function, but such initiatives do apply to the production function.		
Ensuring that office buildings are well insulated and solar powered may help to reduce the running costs of the organisation and also have a positive effect on the environment.		

Task 3.5

It is important that those who work within an accounting function uphold fundamental ethical principles.

The table below details four situations which may arise in business.

Required

(a) From the picklist below, select the fundamental ethical principle that applies in each situation. Note that each option may be used more than once.

Situation	Fundamental ethical principle applicable
You are asked by a colleague to provide the contact details of a client as they were at school together.	▼
You have been asked to complete a VAT return which is a subject you have not yet studied at college and about which you have little knowledge.	▼
Your organisation has a disciplinary and grievance policy which applies to all staff in the organisation, from the most senior partner down.	▼
A new accountant asks you to check an advertisement which is to be placed in the local newspaper. In this he states, 'We are the best accountants in the area and half the price of Jones and Co.'	▼

Picklist

- Confidentiality
- Equality
- Integration
- Objectivity
- Professional behaviour
- Professional competence
- Professional compliance
- Subjectivity

Conflicts of interest may arise during your work as an accountant. It is important you act correctly when they occur.

Required

(b) Review each of the following situations and select the most appropriate course of action from the options provided.

(i) Whilst conducting a year-end audit at a client's business, the client offers to take you on an all-expenses paid holiday to her villa in Spain once you have finished the year-end work.

	✓
Politely decline the offer and do not tell anyone about it.	
Politely accept the offer but ask the client not to mention the holiday to any other members of the audit team.	
Politely accept the offer and work extremely hard to finish the year-end work.	
Politely decline the offer and discuss the situation with your manager.	

(ii) You have been asked to act as an interviewer to help assess and select prospective new trainees for your organisation. Your niece has been selected for one of the interviews.

	✓
Complete the work as interviewer but treat each interviewee fairly and do not tell anyone about your connection with one of the applicants.	
Complete the work as interviewer and ensure you are able to help your niece through to the next stage of the recruitment process.	
Refuse to be involved in any aspect of the assessment and selection of prospective trainees but do not explain to your manager why.	
Discuss the situation with your manager to see if you could complete the work, but abstain from being involved in the assessment of your niece.	

(iii) You have been asked by a family friend to advise them of the names of current bidders and details of their offers regarding a contract that they wish to tender for.

	✓
Provide them with the requested details of current bidders and their offers.	
Provide them with the requested details of the names of the bidders, but not the details of their offers.	
Politely decline to provide any details, explaining you are not allowed to disclose such information.	
Provide them with incorrect details of the other bidders' offers.	

Task 3.6

(a) Which of these might (or might be thought to) affect the objectivity of providers of professional accounting services?

	✓
Failure to keep up-to-date on CPD	
A personal financial interest in the client's affairs	
Being negligent or reckless with the accuracy of the information provided to the client	

(b) Identify which TWO of the following stakeholders a trainee in the accounting function is most likely to communicate with on a regular basis.

Complete the answer by selecting the correct stakeholders from the picklist provided.

Stakeholders an accounting trainee is most likely to communicate with on a regular basis
▼
▼

Picklist

- Chairperson of the local AAT branch
- Government ministers
- HM Revenue & Customs
- People living close to the organisation's offices
- Trade receivables
- Trade union representative

 BPP

Assessment objective 4 – Introduction to bookkeeping/The business environment

Task 4.1

There are three payments to be entered in the credit side of Gold's cash book during one week.

Cash purchases listing

Suppliers paid in cash	Net £	VAT £	Gross £
Mendip plc	315	63	378

Trade payables listing

Credit suppliers paid by cheque	Amount paid £
Landa Ltd	1,950
Bebe and Co	726

Required

(a) Enter the details from the cash purchases listing and the trade payables listing into the credit side of the cash book shown below and total each column.

Cash book – credit side

Details	Cash £	Bank £	VAT £	Trade payables £	Cash purchases £
Balance b/f		2,312			
▼					
▼					
▼					
Total					

Picklist

- Bank
- Bebe and Co
- Cash
- Cash purchases
- Landa Ltd
- Mendip plc
- Trade payables
- VAT

The debit side of the cash book shows the cash balance brought forward at the beginning of the week was £200 and a further £319 has been received during the week.

Required

(b) Using your answer to (a) above, calculate the cash balance.

£ [   ]

The debit side of the cash book shows the total amount of money banked during the week was £1,964.

Required

(c) Using your answer to (a) above, calculate the bank balance. If your calculations show that the bank account is overdrawn, your answer should start with a minus sign, eg –123.

£ [   ]

Task 4.2

Gold's cash book is both a book of prime entry and part of the double entry bookkeeping system. These are the totals of the columns in the credit side of the cash book at the end of a month.

Cash-book – credit side

Details	Cash	Bank	VAT	Trade payables	Cash purchases	Bank charges
	£	£	£	£	£	£
Totals	1,590	10,948	265	10,900	1,325	48

Required

(a) What will be the FOUR entries in the general ledger?

General ledger

Account name	Amount £	Debit ✓	Credit ✓
▼			
▼			
▼			
▼			

Picklist

- Bank
- Bank charges
- Cash
- Cash purchases
- Cash sales
- Details
- Payables ledger control account
- Receivables ledger control
- Totals
- Trade payables
- VAT

One of the bank payments to trade payables was to 'D B Franks' for £264.

Required

(b) What will be the entry in the payables ledger?

Payables ledger

Account name	Amount £	Debit ✓	Credit ✓
▼			

Picklist

- Bank
- D B Franks
- Gold
- Payables ledger
- Payables ledger control
- Purchases
- Receivables ledger
- Receivables ledger control
- Sales
- Trade payables

Task 4.3

The following account is in the receivables ledger at the close of day on 30 June.

Required

Insert the balance carried down together with date and details.

Insert the totals.

Insert the balance brought down together with date and details.

J B Mills

Date 20XX	Details	Amount £	Date 20XX	Details	Amount £
1 Jun	Balance b/f	1,585	22 Jun	Bank	678
11 Jun	Invoice 1269	1,804	29 Jun	Credit note 049	607
▼	▼		▼	▼	
	Total			Total	
▼	▼		▼	▼	

Picklist

- 1 Jul
- 30 Jun
- Balance b/d
- Balance c/d

 BPP

- Gold
- J B Mills

Task 4.4

(a) For each of the following transactions, state whether they are cash or credit transactions.

	Cash transaction ✓	Credit transaction ✓
Purchase of goods for £500 payable by cash in one week's time		
Arranging a bank draft for the purchase of a new computer		
Sale of goods to a customer on account		
Sale of goods to a customer who paid by credit card at time of transaction		
Purchase of goods where payment is due in three week's time		

On your desk is a pile of sales invoices that have already had the price of the goods entered onto them and been totalled.

Required

(b) You now have to calculate and deduct the 15% trade discount that is allowed on each of these invoices.

Goods total £	Trade discount £	Net total £
542.60		
107.50		
98.40		
257.10		
375.00		

(c) There is a further pile of invoices which have the net total entered for which you are required to calculate the VAT charge at 20% and the invoice total.

Net total £	VAT £	Gross total £
236.40		
372.10		
85.60		
159.40		
465.30		

 BPP

Task 4.5

Sugar Solutions is a small business that manufactures a variety of confectionery which it sells directly to shops. During January 20XX, the following credit sales to customers took place:

Invoice No. 7541 to Watsons Ltd £547 plus VAT

Invoice No. 7542 to Harrison £660 plus VAT

Invoice No. 7543 to Valu Shopping £346 plus VAT

Invoice No. 7544 to Fishers £328 plus VAT

Invoice No. 7545 to Harrison £548 plus VAT

Invoice No. 7546 to Villa Discount £141 plus VAT

Invoice No. 7547 to Valu Shopping £416 plus VAT

Invoice No. 7548 to Watsons Ltd £238 plus VAT

Invoice No. 7549 to Fishers £305 plus VAT

Required

(a) Enter these transactions into the sales day book given below.

Sales day book

Customer	Invoice number	Total £	VAT £	Net £
▼				
▼				
▼				
▼				
▼				
▼				
▼				
▼				
▼				
▼				

Picklist

- Fishers
- Harrison
- Valu Shopping
- Villa Discount
- Watsons Ltd

(b) Cast the columns of the sales day book and check that they cross cast.

Cross-cast check

	£
Net	
VAT	
Total	

Task 4.6

You have been given an extract from your organisation's purchases day book in respect of credit transactions taking place in June. No entries have yet been made in the ledgers.

Both suppliers charge VAT on sales.

Required

Complete the purchases day book and state what the entries will be in the payables ledger.

Purchases day book

Date	Details	Invoice number	Total	VAT	Net
20XX			£	£	£
30 June	Bramley Ltd	7623			2,571.00
30 June	Russett & Co	0517	2,400.00		
	Totals				

Payables ledger

Account name	Amount £	Debit ✓	Credit ✓
▼			
▼			

Picklist

- Bramley Ltd
- Net
- Payables ledger control
- Purchases
- Purchases returns
- Receivables ledger control
- Russett & Co
- Sales
- Sales returns
- Total
- VAT

 BPP

Task 4.7

Your organisation has received a statement from a supplier which shows that, as at the end of June 20XX, you owed the supplier £2,876. The payables ledger account for this supplier shows that, at that date, you only owed £1,290.

Required

(a) Which of the following items would explain the difference?

	✓
You have requested a credit note from the supplier for £1,586 which you have not yet received.	
You sent a cheque for £1,586 to the supplier on 30 June 20XX.	
You ordered some items from the supplier on 30 June for £1,586 but the goods have not yet been delivered and an invoice has not yet been raised.	

Matilda sells machine tools. The following is a summary of her transactions with Frampton Ltd, a new credit customer.

£656 re invoice 1540 of 15 September

£742 re invoice 1560 of 29 September

£43 re credit note 89 of 3 October

£1,235 re invoice 1580 of 10 October

Cheque for £682 received 15 October

Required

(b) Complete the statement of account below. Enter all amounts as a positive value.

> **Matilda's Machinery**
> 1 North Street
> **Westbury, WE11 9SD**
> To: Frampton Ltd   Date: 31 October 20XX
>
> | Date | Details | Transaction amount | Outstanding amount |
> |---|---|---|---|
> | 20XX | | £ | £ |
> | | ▼ | | |
> | | ▼ | | |
> | | ▼ | | |
> | | ▼ | | |
> | | ▼ | | |

Picklist

- Cheque
- Credit note 89
- Invoice 1540
- Invoice 1560
- Invoice 1580

Task 4.8

On the first day of every month, cash is drawn from the bank to restore the petty cash imprest level to £75.

A summary of petty cash transactions during November is shown below:

Opening balance on 1 November	£27
Cash from bank on 1 November	£48
Expenditure during month	£21

Required

(a) What will be the amount required to restore the imprest level on 1 December?

£ [   ]

(b) Will the receipt from the bank on 1 December be a debit or credit entry in the petty cash book?

	✓
Debit	
Credit	

Task 4.9

(a) State four benefits of cloud accounting.

(b) State four potential problems of cloud accounting.

Task 4.10

The following are the requirements for the accounting function meeting:

Date: 18 August 20XX	Time: 10:00am–2.00pm	Tea/coffee required: NO Time: N/A	Lunch IS required Time: 12:00
Purpose: The monthly accounting function review meeting			
Number of attendees: 25, plus the finance director and managing director			
Special requirements: Two members of staff require vegetarian food, no other special dietary requirements			
Room configuration: Usual, horseshoe style please			
Other information: We require an overhead projector, white screen and laptop			
Cost to be charged to: Mr John Brean		Budget Code: ACC3217653	

Your manager (John Brean) has asked you to email the facilities manager to advise him of the requirements for the monthly accounting function review meeting.

Required

(a) Complete the email below to book the meeting with the facilities manager, Martin Slone (mslone@Mbs.com) by inserting the email address of the recipient and selecting TWO

 BPP

paragraphs that should be inserted into the main body of the email to make all the arrangements for the meeting.

From:	AATstudent@Mbs.com
To:	
Subject:	Meeting room booking

Hello Martin,

▼

▼

Regards,
AAT student

Picklist

- An overhead projector, white screen and laptop will be required for the meeting. The costs associated with the meeting are to be sent for the attention of John Brean. Budget code ACC3217653 should be charged.

- An overhead projector, white screen and laptop will be required for the meeting. The room should be arranged in our usual style. The costs associated with the meeting are to be sent for the attention of John Brean. Budget code AC3217653 should be charged.

- On behalf of John Brean I write to request a booking for the accounting's function monthly review meeting. There will be 25 staff including the finance director and managing director attending the meeting and lunch will be required at 12:00pm. The only special dietary requirements are that two people require vegetarian food. Tea/coffee will not be required.

- Please arrange for a room to be booked for the accounting function's monthly review meeting. There will be 25 staff plus the finance director and managing director at the meeting between 10:00am and 2:00pm on 18 August 20XX. Tea/coffee will not be required and lunch is requested at 12:00pm. Two people require vegetarian food; there are no dietary requirements.

- The accounting function needs a room for its monthly review meeting on 18 August 20XX. The meeting is due to start at 10:00am and should finish at 2:00pm. There will be 25 people at the meeting and we shall require lunch at 12:00pm; two attendees require vegetarian food, nobody else has any special dietary arrangements. There will not be a requirement for tea or coffee.

- The room should be arranged in a horseshoe style and an overhead projector, wide screen and laptop will be required for the meeting. The costs associated with the meeting are to be sent for the attention of John Brean. Budget code AC3217653 should be charged.

- We require a room for our review meeting on 18 August 20XX between 10:00am and 2:00pm. Tea/coffee is not required but lunch is required at 12:00pm. Two people require vegetarian food; the others have no special dietary requirements.

- We will require an overhead projector, white screen and laptop for the meeting. The room should be arranged in our usual horseshoe style. The costs associated with the meeting are to be sent for the attention of John Brean. Budget code ACC3217653 should be charged.

(b) **Identify whether the following statements are true or false.**

You do not need to proofread emails as this is an informal method of communication.

[▼]

When deciding upon the best method of communication, you only need to consider the

information you are trying to communicate. [▼]

Picklist

- False
- True

Task 4.11

This is a draft of a letter to be addressed to Mrs Oboh, a supplier, to advise her of the results of your reconciliation of the statement of account you received from her. The differences are as follows:

Transaction date	Amount	Comment
12.10.XX	£794.35	The invoice for this entry has been located; however, the invoice total is £749.35.
26.10.XX	£375.29	We have no record of ever ordering or receiving goods to this value from Mrs Oboh.

October Statment Reconciliation

Date: 1/11/XY

Dear Mrs Oboh,

Many thanks for providing the October statement which we have now reviewed and compared to our records of amounts owing by you. We would like too highlight two discrepancies:

(1)   Your entry for £794.53 on 12.01.XX does not corespond with the invoice we have for that date. The invoice shows an amount of £749.35 for these goods.

(2)   Your entry for £357.29 on 26.10.XX is not known to us. We have no record of ever ordering or sending this amount of goods on this date.

Please investigate these differences as we want to be sure our records agree before we setle our account with you. If you would prefer to contact me by telephone to discuss this matter, please do so as we would like to resolve these differences as soon as posible.

Yours sincerely,

_____

Required

Review the draft letter and identify 12 words or collections of letters or digits which are either spelt incorrectly, missing, are inappropriate or are technically incorrect.

Task 4.12

(a) Identify which TWO of the following would occur before the introduction section of a business report.

	✓
Appendices	
Recommendations	
Main body	
Conclusion	
Executive summary	
Title	

(b) Identify which ONE of the following describes the contents of the 'main body' section of a business report.

	✓
Provides suggested actions to overcome the problems identified	
Provides an analysis of the results of the research	
Summarises the main points of the research and analysis	
Provides suggested actions to be taken in the future	

(c) Complete the following statement by selecting the most appropriate answer from the picklist.

When considering the order of a formal business report, which section will usually appear

between the executive summary and the main body?

Picklist

- Appendices
- Conclusions
- Introduction
- Title

Task 4.13

What would be the most appropriate method of communication in each of the following circumstances? Choose from the picklist below.

(1) Explaining to a customer that a prompt payment discount that has been deducted was not valid, as the invoice was not paid within the discount period ▼

(2) Requesting customer balances from a colleague in the receivables ledger department ▼

(3) Providing negative feedback to a colleague on the quality of their work ▼

(4) A formal complaint to a supplier regarding the delivery times of goods, which are not as agreed [▼]

(5) Information to be provided to the sales director regarding the breakdown of sales geographically for the last two years Information to be provided to the sales director regarding the breakdown of sales geographically for the last two years [▼]

Picklist

- Email
- Face-to-face discussion
- Letter
- Telephone

Task 4.14

(a) **For which ONE of the following could a spreadsheet be used?**

	✓
Maintaining detailed customer records	
Preparing budgets and forecasts	
Sending out supplier statements	

(b) **Which THREE of the following are true regarding spreadsheets?**

	✓
Spreadsheets are used to store and manipulate data.	
Spreadsheets can be used for word processing.	
Data in a spreadsheet can be easily updated.	
Spreadsheet data can be output in the form of graphs.	
Spreadsheets can be used to replace accounting packages.	
Sophisticated databases are making spreadsheets obsolete.	

Assessment objective 5 – Principles of bookkeeping controls

Task 5.1

Dee Designs has just started in business, and a new set of accounts is to be opened. A partially completed journal to record the opening entries is shown below.

Required

Complete the journal by showing whether each amount will be a debit or a credit entry.

The Journal

Account name	Amount £	Debit ✓	Credit ✓
Capital	4,780		
Office expenses	1,927		
Sales	8,925		
Purchases	4,212		
Commission received	75		
Discounts received	54		
Cash at bank	1,814		
Petty cash	180		
Bank loan	5,000		
Motor expenses	372		
Motor vehicles	9,443		
Other expenses	886		
Journal to record opening entries of the new business.			

Task 5.2

A payment through the bank of £12,265 for new computer equipment has been entered in the accounting records as £12,565. (Ignore VAT.)

Required

(a) Record the journal entries needed in the general ledger to remove the incorrect entry.

Account name	Amount £	Debit ✓	Credit ✓
▼			
▼			

Picklist

• Bank

• Cash

- Computer equipment
- Purchases
- Suspense

(b) Record the journal entries needed in the general ledger to record the correct entry.

Account name	Amount £	Debit ✓	Credit ✓
▼			
▼			

Picklist

- Bank
- Cash
- Computer equipment
- Purchases
- Suspense

Task 5.3

A company's trial balance includes a suspense account. All of the bookkeeping errors have now been traced and the journal entries shown below have been recorded.

Journal entries

Account name	Debit £	Credit £
Commission received	545	
Rent received		545
Suspense	985	
Legal fees		985
General repairs	3,667	
Suspense		3,667

Required

Post the journal entries to the general ledger accounts below by selecting the details and amounts from the picklist.

(a) Commission received

Details	Amount £	Details	Amount £
▼	▼	▼	▼

(b) Rent received

 BPP

Details	Amount £	Details	Amount £
▼	▼	▼	▼

(c) Suspense

Details	Amount £	Details	Amount £
Balance b/f	2,682	▼	▼
▼	▼		

(d) Legal fees

Details	Amount £	Details	Amount £
▼	▼	▼	▼

(e) General repairs

Details	Amount £	Details	Amount £
▼	▼	▼	▼

Picklist

- 3,667
- 545
- 985
- Commission received
- General repairs
- Legal fees
- Rent received
- Suspense

Task 5.4

A bank statement and cash book for September are shown below.

Bank statement

Date 20XX	Details	Paid out £	Paid in £	Balance £
01 Sep	Balance b/f			4,104 D
01 Sep	BACS transfer – CDL Ltd		4,996	
01 Sep	Cheque 001499	1,015		123 D
04 Sep	Transfer		2,240	2,117 C
12 Sep	Cheque 001500	486		1,631 C

Date	Details	Paid out	Paid in	Balance
20XX		£	£	£
22 Sep	CHAPS transfer – Conway Legal		37,400	
22 Sep	Cheque 001505	819		38,212 C
27 Sep	Cheque 001501	209		
27 Sep	Transfer		1,081	
27 Sep	Cheque 001504	1,618		37,466 C
D = Debit C = Credit				

Cash book

Date	Details	Bank	Date	Cheque Number	Details	Bank
20XX		£	20XX			£
01 Sep	CDL Ltd	4,996	01 Sep		Balance b/f	5,119
04 Sep	Gifford Ltd	2,240	02 Sep	001500	Babbing Ltd	486
22 Sep	Kington Ltd	3,970	08 Sep	001501	Vym plc	209
22 Sep	Conway Legal	37,400	12 Sep	001502	Newton West	195
27 Sep	Fairway Ltd	1,081	12 Sep	001503	Welland Ltd	234
			18 Sep	001504	Hawes Ltd	1,618
			18 Sep	001505	Halthorpe Ltd	819
			18 Sep	001506	Roman plc	316

Required

Identify the **FOUR** transactions that are included in the cash book but missing from the bank statement and complete the bank reconciliation statement below as at 30 September.

Bank reconciliation statement as at 30 September 20XX	£
Balance as per bank statement	
Add:	
▼	
Total to add	
Less:	
▼	
▼	
▼	
Total to subtract	
Balance as per cash book	

Picklist

- Babbing Ltd
- Balance b/f
- Balance c/d
- CDL Ltd
- Cheque 001499
- Conway Legal
- Fairway Ltd
- Gifford Ltd
- Halthorpe Ltd
- Hawes Ltd
- Kington Ltd
- Newton West
- Roman plc
- Vym plc
- Welland Ltd

Task 5.5

The following is a summary of transactions with credit customers during the month of July.

Required

(a) Show whether each entry will be a debit or credit in the receivables ledger control account in the general ledger.

Receivables ledger control account

Details	Amount £	Debit ✓	Credit ✓
Balance owing from credit customers at 1 July	101,912		
Money received from credit customers	80,435		
Irrecoverable debts	228		
Goods sold to credit customers	70,419		
Goods returned by credit customers	2,237		

The following is a summary of transactions with credit suppliers during the month of July.

Required

(b) Show whether each entry will be a debit or credit in the payables ledger control account in the general ledger.

Payables ledger control account

Details	Amount £	Debit ✓	Credit ✓
Balance owing to credit suppliers at 1 July	61,926		
Journal debit to correct an error	550		
Goods returned to credit suppliers	1,128		
Purchases from credit suppliers	40,525		
Payments made to credit suppliers	45,763		

At the beginning of September, the following balances were in the receivables ledger.

Credit customers	Balances	
	Amount £	Debit/Credit
CTC Ltd	11,122	Debit
J B Estates	8,445	Debit
Koo Designs	23,119	Debit
PJB Ltd	1,225	Credit
Probyn plc	19,287	Debit
Yen Products	4,302	Debit

Required

(c) What should be the balance of the receivables ledger control account in order for it to reconcile with the total of the balances in the receivables ledger?

	✓
Credit balance b/d on 1 September of £65,050	
Debit balance b/d on 1 September of £65,050	
Credit balance b/d on 1 September of £67,500	
Debit balance b/d on 1 September of £67,500	

(d) Show whether each of the following statements is true or false.

Statements	True ✓	False ✓
The payables ledger control account enables a business to identify how much is owing to credit suppliers in total.		
The total of the balances in the payables ledger should reconcile with the balance of the receivables ledger control account.		

 BPP

Task 5.6

Below is a summary of transactions to be recorded in the VAT control account.

Transactions	Amount £
VAT owing from HM Revenue and Customs at 1 June	13,146
VAT total in the purchases day book	19,220
VAT total in the sales day book	31,197
VAT total in the purchases returns day book	2,465
VAT total in the sales returns day book	1,779
VAT on cash sales	1,910
VAT on petty cash payments	98
VAT refund received from HM Revenue and Customs	7,131
VAT on irrecoverable debts written off	950
VAT on the sale of office equipment	200

Required

(a) **Show how each of the transactions will be recorded in the VAT control account in the general ledger by inputting each transaction using the picklist below to the appropriate side of the VAT control account.**

VAT control

Details	Amount £	Details	Amount £
▼	▼	▼	▼
▼	▼	▼	▼
▼	▼	▼	▼
▼	▼	▼	▼
▼	▼	▼	▼

Picklist

- 1,779
- 1,910
- 13,146
- 19,220
- 2,465
- 200
- 31,197
- 7,131
- 950
- 98
- Balance b/f – owing from HMRC

- Cash sales
- Irrecoverable debts
- Office equipment sold
- Petty cash
- Purchases
- Purchases returns
- Sales
- Sales returns
- VAT refund

The VAT return shows there is an amount owing from HM Revenue and Customs of £7,710.

Required

(b) Does the balance on the VAT control account in part (a) also show that £7,710 is owing from HM Revenue and Customs?

	✓
Yes	
No	

(c) Identify which ONE of the following sentences is true.

	✓
The VAT control account is used to record the VAT amount of transactions and to help prepare the VAT return.	
The VAT control account is used to record the VAT amount of transactions but has no connection with the VAT return.	

Task 5.7

Your organisation is not registered for VAT.

This is a summary of transactions with credit customers during April.

	£
Balance owing at 1 April	27,321
Goods sold	11,267
Goods returned	1,934
Payments received by cheque	10,006
Irrecoverable debts	742

Required

(a) Record these transactions in the receivables ledger control account and show the balance carried down.

Receivables ledger control

Details	Amount £	Details	Amount £
▼		▼	
▼		▼	
▼		▼	
▼		▼	
▼		▼	

Picklist

- Balance b/f
- Balance c/d
- Bank
- Discounts received
- Irrecoverable debts
- Purchases
- Purchases returns
- Sales
- Sales returns

This is a summary of transactions with credit suppliers for the month of April.

	£
Balance owing at 1 April	6,547
Goods purchased	9,317
Goods returned	751
Payments made by cheque	8,653
Discounts received	481

Required

(b) Record these transactions in the payables ledger control account and show the balance carried down.

Payables ledger control

Details	Amount £	Details	Amount £
▼		▼	
▼		▼	
▼		▼	
▼		▼	

Details	Amount £	Details	Amount £
▼		▼	

Picklist

- Balance b/f
- Balance c/d
- Bank
- Discounts received
- Purchases
- Purchases returns
- Sales
- Sales returns

Task 5.8

(a) When reconciling receivables ledger and payables ledger control accounts to the list of balances from the subsidiary ledgers, would the following errors affect the relevant control account, the list of balances or both?

	Control account ✓	List of balances ✓	Both ✓
Invoice entered into the sales day book as £540 instead of £450			
Purchases day book overcast by £1,100			
An invoice taken as £430 instead of £330 when being posted to the customer's account			
Incorrect balancing of a subsidiary ledger account			
A purchases return not entered into the purchases returns day book			

(b) Would each of the following transactions appear as a payment in or a payment out on a business's bank statement?

Transaction	Payment out ✓	Payment in ✓
£725 paid into the bank		
Direct debit of £47		
Cheque payment of £124.60		
Interest charged on the overdraft		
BACS payment for wages		

 BPP

Task 5.9

The balance on a business's receivables ledger control account at 31 December was £12,467. However, the list of balances in the receivables ledger totalled £11,858. The difference was investigated and the following errors were discovered:

(1) The sales returns day book was undercast by £100.

(2) A payment from one customer had been correctly entered into the cash book as £340 but had been entered into the receivables ledger as £430.

(3) An irrecoverable debt of £250 had been written off in the receivables ledger but had not been entered into the general ledger accounts.

(4) A balance of £169 due from one customer had been omitted from the list of receivables ledger balances.

Required

Write up the corrected receivables ledger control account and to reconcile this to the corrected list of receivables ledger balances.

(a) Receivables ledger control

Details	Amount £	Details	Amount £
▼		▼	
▼		▼	
▼		▼	
▼		▼	
▼		▼	

Picklist

- Balance b/f
- Balance c/d
- Bank
- Discounts received
- Irrecoverable debts
- Purchases
- Purchases returns
- Sales returns

(b) Reconciliation

		£
Receivables ledger list of balances		
Error		
Error		
Amended list of balances		
Amended control account balance		

Task 5.10

A company pays its employees by BACS transfer every month and maintains a wages control account. A summary of last month's payroll transactions is shown below:

Payroll transactions	£
Gross wages	21,999
Income tax	5,755
Employer's NI	1,649
Employees' NI	1,476
Employees' pension contributions	750

Required

(a) Show the journal entries needed in the general ledger to record the wages expense.

Account name	Amount £	Debit ✓	Credit ✓
▼			
▼			

Picklist
- Bank
- Employees' NI
- Employer's NI
- HM Revenue and Customs
- Income tax
- Net wages
- Pension
- Wages control
- Wages expense

(b) Show the journal entries needed in the general ledger to record the net wages paid to employees.

Account name	Amount £	Debit ✓	Credit ✓
▼			
▼			

Picklist
- Bank
- Employees' NI
- Employer's NI
- HM Revenue and Customs

- Income tax
- Net wages
- Pension
- Wages control
- Wages expense

(c) Show which error is an error of omission.

	✓
Recording a bank payment for office expenses on the debit side of the office furniture account.	
Recording a payment for motor expenses in the bank account, the motor expenses account and the miscellaneous expenses account. (Ignore VAT)	
Recording a payment by cheque to a credit supplier in the bank account and payables ledger control account only.	
Recording a cash payment for travel expenses in the cash account only. (Ignore VAT)	

Assessment objective 6 – The business environment

Task 6.1

Charna Ltd contracted with Larma Ltd to buy customised furniture. Delivery was due in May with payment due within 28 days of delivery. In April, Larma Ltd had completed production of the furniture when Charna Ltd emailed to say that it no longer required the furniture and therefore would not send payment.

Required

(a) Which of the following statements are true or false?

Statement	True ✓	False ✓
Charna Ltd will have to pay damages to Larma Ltd even though it notified the company before the delivery date.		
Charna Ltd has committed anticipatory breach of contract.		
Larma Ltd must continue to perform its obligations and deliver the furniture in May.		

(b) Which of the following statements are true or false?

Statement	True ✓	False ✓
In a criminal case, the state is the prosecutor.		
In a criminal case, the prosecutor must prove their case on the balance of probability.		
In a civil case, the burden of proof is on the defendant.		
In a civil case, there is no concept of punishment.		

(c) Match the following statements to the stage in the process of creating legislation.

Statement	Second reading ✓	Report stage ✓
Debate on the general merits of the Bill. No amendments at this stage.		
The Bill as amended in committee is reported to the full House for approval.		

Task 6.2

(a) Identify whether the following statements regarding breach of contract are true or false.

Statement	True ✓	False ✓
Liquidated damages are a genuine pre-estimate of losses that are written into the terms of a contract.		

Statement	True ✓	False ✓
Penalty clauses are an alternative to liquidated damages which courts enforce to punish those in breach on contract.		

(b) Identify whether the following statements regarding consideration are correct or incorrect.

Statement	Correct ✓	Incorrect ✓
Executed consideration is a promise given in return for a promise		
Consideration must be in the form of money to be valid		

(c) Identify whether the following statements regarding acceptance of an offer are true or false.

Statement	True ✓	False ✓
Acceptance of an offer must be in the form of spoken or written words.		
Acceptance may not be made by silence.		
Under the postal rule, acceptance is completed when the letter is delivered to the offeror.		
If acceptance is sent by email, then acceptance is completed when the email is sent.		

Task 6.3

(a) Identify which of the following statements regarding intention to create legal relations are true or false.

Statement	True ✓	False ✓
Intention is not presumed where two spouses are separating.		
Intention is presumed in commercial agreements.		

(b) In which of the following circumstances will an offer be terminated?

Circumstance	Offer terminated ✓	Offer not terminated ✓
The offeree sends a counter offer		
A reasonable time has passed since the offer was made		
There is a failure of a condition of the offer		

Task 6.4

(a) Identify whether the following statements apply to expectation or reliance interest when calculating damages for breach of contract.

Statement	Expectation interest ✓	Reliance interest ✓
The amount awarded as damages is what is needed to compensate the injured party for wasted expenditure due to performing on the contract.		
The amount awarded as damages is what is needed to put the claimant in the position they would have achieved if the contract had been performed.		

(b) Identify whether the following statements concern, void, voidable or unenforceable contracts.

Statement	Void contract ✓	Voidable contract ✓	Unenforceable contract ✓
The contract is valid but performance by one party cannot be enforced			
There is no contract			
The innocent party can withdraw from the contract			

(c) Identify which equitable remedy is described in each statement.

Statement	Rectification ✓	Rescission ✓	Injunction ✓	Specific performance ✓
Restoration of the pre-contract status quo				
The defendant must do what they had agreed to do				
The alteration of a document to reflect the parties' true intentions				
The defendant must abstain from wrongdoing				

Task 6.5

(a) Identify whether the following statements concerning the Consumer Rights Act 2015 are correct.

Statement	Correct ✓	Incorrect ✓
The Act only applies to exclusion clauses.		
A business may be classified as acting as a consumer in some contracts.		
Under the Act, some terms are deemed to be automatically enforceable.		

(b) Identify whether the following statements concerning remedies for breach of contract are correct or incorrect.

Statement	Correct ✓	Incorrect ✓
Damages are a common law remedy.		
Damages are generally only payable for economic losses.		
Equitable remedies are only awarded at the discretion of the court.		

(c) Match the following statements to the correct track in the civil law system.

Statement	Small claims track ✓	Multi-track ✓	Fast track ✓
Hears cases with a value of over £25,000			
Hears cases with a value of between £10,000 and £25,000			
Hears cases with a value of under £10,000			

(d) Rank the following courts in order of their place in the criminal court system hierarchy (1st is the highest court; 5th is the lowest court).

Court	1st ✓	2nd ✓	3rd ✓	4th ✓	5th ✓
Crown court					
Supreme court					
Magistrate's court					
Court of Appeal					
High court					

Assessment objective 7 – The business environment/Introduction to bookkeeping/Principles of Bookkeeping Controls

Task 7.1

(a) What is the retention period for banking records for:

	✓
1 year	
3 years	
6 years	
9 years	

(b) Match the statement to the type of digital financial technology.

Statement	Data analytics ✓	Distributed ledger technology ✓
Technology that allows organisations and individuals who are unconnected to share an agreed record of events, such as ownership of an asset.		
The collection, management and analysis of large data sets (such as big data) with the objective of discovering useful information such as customer buying patterns, that an organisation can use for decision making.		

(c) State THREE business risks associated with sharing computer passwords.

Task 7.2

(a) Using the example of a sale to a customer, explain how a digital system differs from a manual system for recording transactions.

Your answer should refer to the books of prime entry, the receivables ledger and the receivables ledger control account.

This characteristic allows the reader to fully appreciate the information being presented.

 BPP

Required

(b) Which characteristic of useful information does this describe?

	✓
Comparable	
Understandable	
Consistent	
Relevant and reliable	

This characteristic concerns the trustworthiness or accuracy of big data.

Required

(c) Which characteristic of big data does this describe?

	✓
Volume	
Velocity	
Value	
Variety	
Veracity	

Task 7.3

Always using the same methods and policies to calculate figures in financial statements.

Required

(a) Which characteristic of useful information does this describe?

	✓
Comparable	
Understandable	
Consistent	
Relevant and reliable	

(b) State THREE risks to a business that might be caused by a cyberattack.

A cyberattacker sent Monty an email which appeared to be from his bank. The email requested that Monty sent back personal details to 'verify' him. Monty recognised the threat and avoided being a victim of cybercrime.

Required

(c) Which type of cyberattack was used against Monty?

	✓
Pharming	
Hacking	
Phishing	
Keylogging	

Task 7.4

(a) How long should employee records be kept for?

	✓
1 year after leaving employment	
3 years in total	
6 years in total	
9 years in total	

(b) Which type of big data originates from social networks, blogs, emails, text messages and internet searches?

	✓
Processed data	
Open data	
Machine generated data	
Human-sourced data	

Nila runs a business with her brother Zak and ten employees. She is keen to make sure all business data is held safely and securely and is developing some policies for the business covering data security.

Required

(c) State THREE policies that would help make sure all business data is held safely and securely.

Task 7.5

(a) Using the example of a purchase from a supplier, explain how a digital system differs from a manual system for recording transactions.

Your answer should refer to the books of prime entry, the payables ledger and the payables ledger control account.

Information is available when needed.

Required

(b) Which characteristic of useful information is being described?

	✓
Relevant and reliable	
Understandable	
Comparable	
Timely	

Software protection that intercepts data being transmitted in and out of a system.

Required

(c) Which cybersecurity method is being described?

	✓
Access control	
Malware and virus protection	
Boundary firewalls and internet gateways	
Secure configuration	

Task 7.6

(a) Select ONE type of information that will be provided by the accounting department to EACH of the departments from the picklist below.

Department to which the accounting department will provide information	Information
Sales department	▼
Purchasing department	▼

Picklist

- Analysis of cash payments and receipts
- Analysis of sales revenue by region compared to budget
- Details of employee costs
- Discrepancies between supplier invoices and purchase orders

(b) Describe how automation and artificial intelligence can benefit accountants and auditors.

(c) Botnets are used in which type of cyberattack?

	✓
Distributed denial of service (DDoS) attack	
Keylogging	
Screenshot manager	
Ad clicker	

Assessment objective 8 – The business environment

Task 8.1

(a) Identify whether the following statements regarding uncertainty and risk are true or false.

Statement	True ✓	False ✓
Risk is the chance of damage being done to an organisation.		
Businesses cannot avoid uncertainty.		

(b) Are the following taxes revenue or capital taxes?

Tax	Revenue ✓	Capital ✓
Corporation tax		
Inheritance tax		
National insurance		

(c) Identify whether the following statements relate to micro or macro-economics.

Statement	Micro-economics ✓	Macro-economics ✓
Determines how much of a good consumers will buy at a particular price		
Concerned with issues such as taxation and interest rates		
Relates to a specific country		

Task 8.2

(a) Which of the following statements is correct regarding the value of money and inflation?

	✓
The value of money rises as inflation rises	
Inflation does not impact on the value of money	
The value of money will fall as inflation rises	

(b) Which of the following principles of an effective tax system is related to the right amount of tax being generated at the right time?

	✓
Economy	
Fairness	
Equity	

(c) Identify whether the following statements regarding the equilibrium price are true or false.

Statement	True ✓	False ✓
The equilibrium price for a market is always fixed.		
The equilibrium price is the lowest price charged for a good in the market.		
The equilibrium price is the price of a good where the volume demanded and the volume supplied in a market are the same.		

Task 8.3

(a) Identify TWO instruments of monetary policy.

	✓
Government spending	
Interest rates	
Exchange rates	
Taxation	

(b) The demand for which type of good decreases as consumer incomes rise?

	✓
Luxury	
Inferior	
Normal	

(c) Which of the following statements is correct regarding the profit motive?

	✓
Every business organisation is motivated by profit	
Making short-term losses is consistent with the profit motive	
The profit motive describes the purpose of organisations to make the local economy wealthier	

Task 8.4

(a) Identify whether the following are benefits or disadvantages to a business of trading globally.

	Benefit ✓	Disadvantage ✓
Government incentives		
Market size		

BPP

	Benefit ✓	Disadvantage ✓
Logistics		

The PESTEL model is one method of identifying sources of risk and uncertainty.

Required

(b) Which of the following factors does the 'P' in PESTEL relate to?

	✓
Price	
Population	
Political	

(c) Identify whether the following taxes are direct or indirect taxes.

Tax	Direct ✓	Indirect ✓
Capital gains tax		
VAT		
Inheritance tax		

Task 8.5

(a) Identify whether the following factors affect demand or supply of a product.

Factor	Affects demand ✓	Affects supply ✓
Production costs		
Interrelated goods		
Income levels		

(b) Which of the following statements is correct regarding the value of money and deflation?

	✓
Where there is deflation, the value of money will rise.	
Deflation does not affect the value of money.	
Where there is deflation, the value of money will fall.	

(c) Identify TWO instruments of fiscal policy.

	✓
Reserve requirements	
Government spending	
Interest rates	
Taxation	

Answers

Assessment objective 1 – The business environment

Task 1.1

(a) The correct answers are:

Statement	True ✓	False ✓
Sole traders do not have to share their profits with anyone.	✓	
A sole trader has complete control over the business.	✓	
Sole traders may employ staff.	✓	

Sole traders are free to run the business themselves as they see fit, and all profits accrue to them. They may employ staff if they wish.

(b) The correct answers are:

Statement	True ✓	False ✓
Accounts of business entities reflect the financial position of the owners.		✓
The entity concept means that the owners of the business must be separate from those who manage it.		✓
Not all business entities have limited liability.	✓	

The entity concept allows the separation of business ownership from management, but this does not always have to be the case. Accounts of business entities should only reflect the performance and financial position of the business.

Not all business entities have limited liability (for example, traditional partnerships).

(c) The correct answers are:

Statement	True ✓	False ✓
An unlimited company can be a private or public company.		✓
An unlimited company is not usually required to file a copy of its annual accounts and reports with the Registrar each year.	✓	

An unlimited company can only be a private company.

An unlimited company is not usually required to file a copy of its annual accounts and reports with the Registrar each year.

 BPP

Task 1.2

(a) The correct answer is:

	✓
Logistics	✓
Operations	
Marketing	

(b) The correct answer is:

	✓
Marketing	✓
Finance	
Information technology	

(c) The correct answer is:

	✓
Operations	✓
Information technology	
Logistics	

(d) The correct answers are:

Statement	True ✓	False ✓
An entity is a legal concept.	✓	
The financial accounts of an entity should only reflect the entity's business activities and financial performance.	✓	
An entity is a part of a business.		✓

The entity concept applies to a whole business, not business functions. It is a legal concept that allows, for example, a business to own its assets and be liable for its debts. An entity's financial accounts should only reflect its own business activities and its financial performance - not those of its owners.

(e) The correct answers are:

Statement	True ✓	False ✓
'Passing off' actions are used when a company takes another to court to dispute their use of a company name.	✓	
Companies can complain about the use of a name by another company to the Registrar of Companies.		✓

A company or person who considers that their rights have been infringed can apply for an injunction to restrain a company from using a company name. It can do this through a 'passing off' action.

Complaints about company names go to the Company Names Adjudicator.

Task 1.3

(a) The correct answer is:

	✓
Memorandum of association	
Articles of association	✓
Statement of compliance	

If Articles of association are not submitted to the Registrar, the company will be formed with model articles.

(b) The correct answers are:

Statement	True ✓	False ✓
A company's shareholders jointly own the business's assets.		✓
A company must employ directors who are not the business's owners.		✓
A company is liable for its debts.	✓	

As a separate legal entity, the company owns its assets and is the only party liable for its debts.

There is nothing stopping directors from also being the company's owners (shareholders).

(c) The correct answer is:

	✓
Marketing	
Operations	✓
Human resources	

(d) The correct answer is:

	✓
Human resources	✓
Finance	
Logistics	

(e) The correct answer is:

	✓
Operations	
Marketing	✓
Finance	

Task 1.4

(a) The correct answers are:

Statement	True ✓	False ✓
Partners have the right to be involved in managing the partnership unless agreed otherwise.	✓	
Partners are deemed to share profits equally unless agreed otherwise.	✓	
Forming a limited liability partnership (LLP) is where the partners simply agree to run a business together.		✓

Forming an LLP requires documents to be submitted to the Registrar of Companies. Unless agreed otherwise, partners have an equal stake in the profits of the firm and are to be involved in managing the partnership.

(b) The correct answer is:

	✓
Human resources	
Logistics	
Sales and marketing	✓

(c) The correct answer is:

	✓
Operations	
Finance	✓
Sales and marketing	

(d) The correct answer is:

	✓
Finance	
Human resources	✓
Operations	

(e) The correct answer is:

	✓
Upskilling	
Outsourcing	✓
Contracting out	

Outsourcing a business process involves finding an outsource partner to provide the service and then drawing up a contract containing the terms of the arrangement such as the service to be provided and the fee to be paid. Once up and running, the organisation just lets the partner get on with providing the service.

Task 1.5

(a) The correct answers are:

Statement	True ✓	False ✓
Setting up a business as a company limited by guarantee means that business owners have to place money in a ring-fenced account which guarantees a sum of money is always available to pay the company's debts.		✓
A company can only raise money by selling shares if it is a public limited company.		✓
Close family are permitted to form partnerships if they wish.	✓	

There is nothing in law preventing close family from setting up as a partnership.

Companies limited by guarantee do not have share capital and the members only have to contribute what they have guaranteed in the event of a winding up (no ring-fenced account is required).

Private companies can also raise finance by selling shares, they just cannot sell the shares publicly.

(b) The correct answer is:

	✓
'Off-the-shelf' companies are usually formed with unique Articles of association.	
Purchasing an 'off-the-shelf' company means that the new owners do not have to file registration documents with the Registrar.	✓
Buying an 'off-the-shelf' company to avoid liability for pre-incorporation expenses does not work.	

As 'off-the-shelf' companies have already been formed, no registration documents need to be filed and there is no risk of liability for pre-incorporation expenses. Such companies are usually formed with model Articles of association (so they are not unique).

(c) The correct answer is:

	✓
Corporation tax	✓
VAT	
Inheritance tax	

Companies pay corporation tax and are not subject to inheritance tax. They only have to account for and pay VAT if they meet the qualifying threshold.

Assessment objective 2 – The business environment

Task 2.1

(a) The correct answers are:

	✓
The business may have insufficient funds available to pay a debt becoming payable next week.	✓
You will not be able to complete the work for your line manager.	
You will be able to complete the work for your line manager.	✓
The money will not have to be banked by someone else.	

(b) The most appropriate action to take is:

> Explain the situation to your manager and try to find a solution.

(c)

Wednesday To-do list	Order of task completion
Collect and distribute post	First task
Calculate depreciation and process the related journals	Second task
Briefing from managing director	Third task
Enter cash payments and receipts	Fourth task
Receivables reconciliation	Fifth task
Supplier statement reconciliations	Sixth task

This results in the following timetable and ensures all tasks are completed on time:

Task/break	Duration (hrs)	Task order	Time period
Collect and distribute post	0.5	First task	09:30–10:00
Calculate depreciation and process the related journals	1.5	Second task	10:00–11:30
Briefing from Managing Director	1	Third task	11:30–12:30
LUNCH	1		12:30–13:30
Enter cash payments and receipts	3	Fourth task	13:30–16:30
Receivables reconciliation	0.75	Fifth task	16:30–17:15
*Supplier statement reconciliations	0.25 (of 1)	Sixth task	17:15–17:30*

*Starting this task will mean it can be completed before the deadline on Thursday since there will only be 45 more minutes' worth of work to do on Thursday morning.

 BPP

Task 2.2

Monday To-do list	Time
Departmental reports	09:00–10:00
Accounting function meeting	10:00–11:00
Departmental reports	11:00–12:00
Lunch	12:00–13:00
Variance report	13:00–14:00
Wages analysis	14:00–15:00
Wages analysis	15:00–16:00
Wages analysis	16:00–17:00

Task 2.3

(a) The correct answer is:

	✓
Production quality control policy	
Website development procedures	
Staff code of behaviour policy	✓
Motor vehicle maintenance policy	

(b) The correct answers are:

	✓
Organisations, by law, must have at least ten policies and procedures.	
It is good practice for organisations to have policies and procedures so all staff work to a consistent standard.	✓
Data protection policy is an example of a policy that would not apply to those staff working in an accounting function.	
Organisational procedures always result in staff taking longer to do work tasks.	
Ensuring staff adhere to organisational policies and procedures should result in more efficient working practices.	✓
The health and safety policy only applies to those working in the production department.	

(c) This policy has been compiled to aid compliance with data protection legislation.

Task 2.4

(a) The correct answer is:

	✓
Complete the additional task as your manager is the most senior person you work for, then do whatever other work you can. The colleague will have to wait for their work until you have time to complete it.	
Complete the additional task as your manager is the most senior person you work for, then do whatever other work you can. You will prioritise the colleague's work for the next day.	
Complete the colleague's work as they asked you to do the work first and you will start the manager's work tomorrow.	
Discuss your workload with both the manager and the colleague to decide on the work priority and renegotiate deadlines where appropriate.	✓

(b) The correct answers are:

Statement	True ✓	False ✓
There will be no impact. If you cannot check supplier statements on Thursday, you can prioritise this work the next day.		✓
Your colleague may be unable to pay suppliers by the due date which may result in problems for the organisation in receiving future supplies.	✓	

(c)

Action	Contributes to:
Reduce customer credit terms so they pay their debts earlier	The management of working capital and solvency
Ensure IT support is in place in case staff encounter computer problems	The smooth running of the business
Produce a health and safety policy to be circulated to all staff	Compliance with applicable laws and regulations
Ensure all staff are paid at least the minimum wage	Compliance with applicable laws and regulations
Ensure staff recruited for each job have the relevant experience and skills	The smooth running of the business
Avoid the build-up of surplus inventories	The management of working capital and solvency

Task 2.5

(a)

Order	Task
1st task (10:00am–12:00pm)	Enter sales invoices/credit notes into computer system
2nd task (12:00pm–1:00pm)	Enter weekly purchase invoices into the computer
3rd task (2:00pm–4:00pm) (20 × 6 mins = 120 mins)	Match purchase invoices to goods received notes and pass to the accountant for authorisation
4th task (4:00pm–5:00pm)	Filing

(b) The correct answers are:

	✓
Maximise inventory levels	
Issue statements to trade receivables on a regular basis	✓
Pay trade payables as soon as invoices are received	
Encourage trade receivables to pay the amounts owed on or before the due date	✓
Ensure the organisation has a staff development policy	
Issue statements to trade payables on a regular basis	

Task 2.6

(a) The correct answer is:

	✓
The directors	✓
The shareholders	
The internal auditors	
The management accountants	

(b) The correct answer is:

	✓
The finance director	
The management accountants	✓
The external auditor	
The board of directors	

The directors are responsible for the statutory financial statements. The management accountants are responsible for providing costing information, including variance analysis.

 BPP

(c) The correct answers are:

Information	Internal ✓	External ✓
Employee salaries	✓	
Tax rates		✓

Employee salaries will come from HR or payroll. Tax rates would be sourced externally, for example from a Government website.

(d) The correct answers are:

Statement	True ✓	False ✓
An advantage of secondary information is that the investigator knows where the information has come from.		✓
A disadvantage of secondary information is that the investigator may not be aware of any inadequacies or limitations in the information.	✓	

Secondary information is not collected by the investigator themselves. Therefore, they may be unaware of the source as well as any inadequacies or limitations of it.

Task 2.7

(a) The correct answer is:

	✓
The financial accountants	
The shareholders	
The external auditors	✓
The internal auditors	

(b) The correct answer is:

	✓
The financial accountants	✓
The management accountants	
The finance director	
The human resources function	

The external auditors sign an audit report after verifying the accounts show a true and fair view. The recording of expenses, such as salaries, is performed by the financial accountants.

(c) The correct answers are:

Information supplied	Sales and marketing ✓	Logistics ✓
Details of inventory counts		✓
VAT rates on different products and services	✓	
Credit notes issued to customers	✓	

Logistics are responsible for storing and moving materials and finished goods. Therefore, information on inventory counts should be sent there. Sales and marketing need to know VAT rates to help with pricing decisions and credit notes to ensure customer accounts are kept up-to-date.

(d) The correct answers are:

	✓
Concise	✓
Measurable	
Efficient	
Planned	
Compliant	
Complete	✓

The principles of effective communication are complete, accurate, timely and concise.

Task 2.8

(a) The correct answers are:

Policy	Function-specific policy ✓	Organisation-wide policy ✓
Financial controls policy	✓	
Equal opportunities policy		✓

A financial controls policy would be specific to functions in the finance area. An equal opportunities policy would apply throughout the organisation.

(b) The correct answers are:

Statement	Management accounts ✓	Statutory financial accounts ✓
Not regulated by law	✓	
Filed with the Registrar of Companies		✓

Management accounts are purely internal documents and are not regulated by law.

 BPP

Statutory financial accounts must comply with the law and are usually filed with the Registrar of Companies.

(c) The correct answers are:

	✓
Routine	
Urgent	✓
Unexpected	✓

The task is not routine because it is not included in your job description. It is urgent because it is needed today. It is unexpected because it falls outside of your routine tasks.

Assessment objective 3 – The business environment

Task 3.1

(a) The correct answers are:

Statement	True ✓	False ✓
Those working within an accounting environment do not need to act with integrity.		✓
Personal information of a client cannot be given to other people unless the client authorises it.	✓	
Information about the income generated by a client listed on the stock exchange can be discussed with your friends as, at the end of the year, the organisation will publish its financial results.		✓
A conflict of interest never has to be declared if the employee feels happy about the situation.		✓

(b) The correct answers are:

	✓
Hold all meetings face-to-face rather than virtually.	
Have all corridor, hall and passage lighting linked to motion sensors so they automatically switch off when no one is using them.	✓
Always select the most competitively priced suppliers of goods and services.	
Ensure all qualified accountants complete CPD.	
Do business with any organisations regardless of their environmental practices.	
Ensure costs and expenses are minimised in every instance.	
Arrange monthly management meetings virtually rather than at head office.	✓
Encourage employees to print out emails.	

(c) Corporate social responsibility (CSR) is a business practice that involves participating in initiatives that benefit society. As consumers become more aware about global social issues, they look at an organisation's CSR when deciding where to spend their money. CSR is now also increasingly a factor which attracts talented people when they are choosing where to work.

A primary focus of CSR is the environment. Businesses should seek to reduce their carbon footprint and consider issues of pollution and depletion of the earth's resources. Many organisations donate time or money to charities as part of their CSR. CSR also demands ethical labour practices, particularly in relation to employees in overseas locations.

 BPP

Task 3.2

(a)

Fundamental ethical principles
Objectivity
Confidentiality
Integrity

(b) Ethics is a set of moral principles that guides personal behaviour and must also guide behaviour in business.

Professional behaviour is one of the fundamental principles in the AAT Code of Ethics. It requires an AAT member to comply with the law and avoid any action that brings the profession into disrepute.

The confidentiality of information acquired as a result of professional and business relationships must be respected. This is an important part of the relationship of trust which must exist with colleagues and clients. You should not use or disclose confidential information unless you are properly authorised to do so or have a legal or professional right or duty to disclose.

An accounts department can be dealing with the financial affairs of a company or the financial affairs of clients. In either situation, accounting staff are trusted to produce accurate financial information and to safeguard the interests of the company or the clients. This requires them to maintain high ethical standards and avoid conflicts of interest.

Task 3.3

(a) The correct answers are:

	✓
Introduce a waste recycling scheme	✓
Recruit only fully trained staff	
Use video conferencing to save staff having to travel to team meetings	✓
Increase prices every time costs go up	
Obtain goods and services from the cheapest supplier	
Give all staff a pay rise every year	
Introduce procedures to ensure that all electrical equipment is fully switched off each day when the office is vacated	✓
Encourage staff not to print emails unless absolutely necessary	✓

(b) The correct answers are:

Statement	True ✓	False ✓
Sustainability means ensuring the organisation focuses purely on economic growth at all costs.		✓

Statement	True ✓	False ✓
Encouraging suppliers to send electronic invoices can be part of an organisation's sustainability agenda.	✓	
When sourcing goods and services, an organisation should check that potential suppliers have good environmental policies.	✓	
Planning the routes of delivery vehicles to minimise distance travelled may reduce the running costs of the organisation and also have a positive effect on the environment.	✓	

Task 3.4

(a) The correct answers are:

	✓
Arrange virtual rather than face-to-face team meetings	✓
Have all office lighting linked to motion sensors so they automatically switch off when the office is empty	✓
Always select the lowest priced suppliers of goods and services	
Ensure all trainee accountants complete CPD	
Do business only with organisations which can demonstrate they follow responsible environmental practices	✓
Ensure costs and expenses are minimised in every instance	
Arrange monthly management meetings at a central point in the country rather than at head office	
Restrict paper usage to the printing of essential documents only	✓

(b) The correct answers are:

Statement	True ✓	False ✓
Sustainability means ensuring the organisation focuses purely on generating the highest profit irrespective of the consequences of the organisation's actions.		✓
When building new premises, trying to ensure the building is carbon neutral even if this results in increased initial costs is an example of a sustainable initiative by the organisation.	✓	
Sustainable initiatives do not apply to those in an accounting function, but such initiatives do apply to the production function.		✓

Statement	True ✓	False ✓
Ensuring that office buildings are well insulated and solar powered may help to reduce the running costs of the organisation and also have a positive effect on the environment.	✓	

Task 3.5

(a)

Situation	Fundamental ethical principle applicable
You are asked by a colleague to provide the contact details of a client as they were at school together.	Confidentiality
You have been asked to complete a VAT return which is a subject you have not yet studied at college and about which you have little knowledge.	Professional competence
Your organisation has a disciplinary and grievance policy which applies to all staff in the organisation, from the most senior partner down.	Professional behaviour
A new accountant asks you to check an advertisement which is to be placed in the local newspaper. In this he states, 'We are the best accountants in the area and half the price of Jones and Co.'	Professional behaviour

(b) (i) The correct answer is:

	✓
Politely decline the offer and do not tell anyone about it.	
Politely accept the offer but ask the client not to mention the holiday to any other members of the audit team.	
Politely accept the offer and work extremely hard to finish the year-end work.	
Politely decline the offer and discuss the situation with your manager.	✓

 BPP

(ii) The correct answer is:

	✓
Complete the work as interviewer but treat each interviewee fairly and do not tell anyone about your connection with one of the applicants.	
Complete the work as interviewer and ensure you are able to help your niece through to the next stage of the recruitment process.	
Refuse to be involved in any aspect of the assessment and selection of prospective trainees but do not explain to your manager why.	
Discuss the situation with your manager to see if you could complete the work, but abstain from being involved in the assessment of your niece.	✓

(iii) The correct answer is:

	✓
Provide them with the requested details of current bidders and their offers.	
Provide them with the requested details of the names of the bidders, but not the details of their offers.	
Politely decline to provide any details, explaining you are not allowed to disclose such information.	✓
Provide them with incorrect details of the other bidders' offers.	

Task 3.6

(a) The correct answer is:

	✓
Failure to keep up-to-date on CPD	
A personal financial interest in the client's affairs	✓
Being negligent or reckless with the accuracy of the information provided to the client	

A personal financial interest in the client's affairs will affect objectivity. Failure to keep up-to-date on CPD is an issue of professional competence, while providing inaccurate information reflects upon professional integrity.

(b)

Stakeholders an accounting trainee is most likely to communicate with on a regular basis
HM Revenue & Customs
Trade receivables

Assessment objective 4 – Introduction to bookkeeping/The business environment

Task 4.1

(a) Cash book – credit side

Details	Cash £	Bank £	VAT £	Trade payables £	Cash purchases £
Balance b/f		2,312			
Mendip plc	378		63		315
Landa Ltd		1,950		1,950	
Bebe and Co		726		726	
Total	378	4,988	63	2,676	315

(b) £ 141

Working

£200 + £319 – £378

(c) £ -3,024

Working

£1,964 – £4,988

Task 4.2

(a) General ledger

Account name	Amount £	Debit ✓	Credit ✓
VAT	265	✓	
Payables ledger control account	10,900	✓	
Cash purchases	1,325	✓	
Bank charges	48	✓	

(b) Payables ledger

Account name	Amount £	Debit ✓	Credit ✓
D B Franks	264	✓	

 BPP

Task 4.3

J B Mills

Date 20XX	Details	Amount £	Date 20XX	Details	Amount £
1 Jun	Balance b/f	1,585	22 Jun	Bank	678
11 Jun	Invoice 1269	1,804	29 Jun	Credit note 049	607
			30 Jun	Balance c/d	2,104
	Total	3,389		Total	3,389
1 Jul	Balance b/d	2,104			

Task 4.4

(a) The correct answers are:

	Cash transaction ✓	Credit transaction ✓
Purchase of goods for £500 payable by cash in one week's time		✓
Arranging a bank draft for the purchase of a new computer	✓	
Sale of goods to a customer on account		✓
Sale of goods to a customer who paid by credit card at time of transaction	✓	
Purchase of goods where payment is due in three week's time		✓

(b)

Goods total £	Trade discount £	Net total £
542.60	81.39	461.21
107.50	16.13	91.37
98.40	14.76	83.64
257.10	38.57	218.53
375.00	56.25	318.75

Trade discount = 15% × price

(c)

Net total	VAT	Gross total
£	£	£
236.40	47.28	283.68
372.10	74.42	446.52
85.60	17.12	102.72
159.40	31.88	191.28
465.30	93.06	558.36

VAT = Net × 20%

Task 4.5

(a) Sales day book

Customer	Invoice number	Total	VAT	Net
		£	£	£
Watsons Ltd	7541	656.40	109.40	547.00
Harrison	7542	792.00	132.00	660.00
Valu Shopping	7543	415.20	69.20	346.00
Fishers	7544	393.60	65.60	328.00
Harrison	7545	657.60	109.60	548.00
Villa Discount	7546	169.20	28.20	141.00
Valu Shopping	7547	499.20	83.20	416.00
Watsons Ltd	7548	285.60	47.60	238.00
Fishers	7549	366.00	61.00	305.00
		4,234.80	705.80	3,529.00

(b) Cross-cast check

	£
Net	3,529.00
VAT	705.80
Total	4,234.80

BPP

ANSWERS

Task 4.6

Purchases day book

Date	Details	Invoice number	Total	VAT	Net
20XX			£	£	£
30 June	Bramley Ltd	7623	3,085.20	514.20	2,571.00
30 June	Russett & Co	0517	2,400.00	400.00	2,000.00
	Totals		5,485.20	914.20	4,571.00

Payables ledger

Account name	Amount £	Debit ✓	Credit ✓
Bramley Ltd	3,085.20		✓
Russett & Co	2,400.00		✓

Task 4.7

(a) The correct answer is:

	✓
You have requested a credit note from the supplier for £1,586 which you have not yet received.	
You sent a cheque for £1,586 to the supplier on 30 June 20XX.	✓
You ordered some items from the supplier on 30 June for £1,586 but the goods have not yet been delivered and an invoice has not yet been raised.	

(b)

Matilda's Machinery
1 North Street
Westbury, WE11 9SD
To: Frampton Ltd   Date: 31 October 20XX

Date	Details	Transaction amount	Outstanding amount
20XX		£	£
15 September	Invoice 1540	656	656
29 September	Invoice 1560	742	1,398
3 October	Credit note 89	43	1,355
10 October	Invoice 1580	1,235	2,590
15 October	Cheque	682	1,908

Task 4.8

(a) £ 21

Working

	£
Opening balance	27
Cash from bank	48
Less: expenditure during month	(21)
balance at end of month	54

Therefore, £75 – £54 = £21 is required to restore the imprest level.

(b) The correct answer is:

	✓
Debit	✓
Credit	

Task 4.9

(a) The main benefits of a cloud accounting system over a traditional system installed on individual machines include (any four from):

- System data and the software itself is automatically refreshed and kept up-to-date.
- Information in the system is available to multiple users simultaneously and globally, as long as the users have internet access and a login.
- Duplication and other system errors and inconsistencies are eliminated because only one set of data is kept and is synchronised to all users.
- Data is stored in one offsite location and users simply access the information when required. There is no need to transmit the data between users over the internet or by USB stick, increasing data security.
- Multiple users mean key people can access financial and customer details should they need to.
- It reduces the cost and complexity of keeping backups of the data because this is performed by the cloud service provider.
- It reduces the cost and time involved in upgrading the software.
- It improves support and customer service because the service provider can access the user's information to help resolve issues.

(b) The main potential problems of cloud accounting include (any four from the following):

- Increased risk of cyberattacks as the system is online
- Increased risk of loss of, or damage to data
- Reliance on cybersecurity being provided by the service provider
- Reliance on the service provider maintaining back-ups of company data
- Needing to ensure the cloud accounting subscription is maintained to avoid loss of service

 BPP

- Queries regarding payment or other account issues may led to services being withdrawn and data deleted by the service provider

Task 4.10

(a)

From:	AATstudent@Mbs.com
To:	mslone@mbs.com
Subject:	Meeting room booking

Hello Martin,

Please arrange for a room to be booked for the accounting function's monthly review meeting. There will be 25 staff plus the finance director and managing director at the meeting between 10:00am and 2:00pm on 18 August 20XX. Tea/coffee will not be required and lunch is requested at 12:00pm. Two people require vegetarian food; there are no dietary requirements.

We will require an overhead projector, white screen and laptop for the meeting. The room should be arranged in our usual horseshoe style. The costs associated with the meeting are to be sent for the attention of John Brean. Budget code ACC3217653 should be charged.

Regards,

AAT student

(b) You do not need to proofread emails as this is an informal method of communication. | False |

When deciding upon the best method of communication, you only need to consider the information you are trying to communicate. | False |

Task 4.11

October Statment Reconciliation

Date: 1/11/XY

Dear Mrs Oboh,

Many thanks for providing the October statement which we have now reviewed and compared to our records of amounts owing by you. We would like too highlight two discrepancies:

(1) Your entry for £794.53 on 12.01.XX does not corespond with the invoice we have for that date. The invoice shows an amount of £749.35 for these goods.

(2) Your entry for £357.29 on 26.10.XX is not known to us. We have no record of ever ordering or sending this amount of goods on this date.

Please investigate these differences as we want to be sure our records agree before we setle our account with you. If you would prefer to contact me by telephone to discuss this matter, please do so as we would like to resolve these differences as soon as posible.

Yours sincerely,

Task 4.12

(a) The correct answers are:

	✓
Appendices	
Recommendations	
Main body	
Conclusion	
Executive summary	✓
Title	✓

(b) The correct answer is:

	✓
Provides suggested actions to overcome the problems identified	
Provides an analysis of the results of the research	✓
Summarises the main points of the research and analysis	
Provides suggested actions to be taken in the future	

(c) When considering the order of a formal business report, which section will usually appear between the executive summary and the main body?

Introduction

Task 4.13

(1) Explaining to a customer that a prompt payment discount that has been deducted was not valid, as the invoice was not paid within the discount period   Telephone

(2) Requesting customer balances from a colleague in the receivables ledger department   Email

(3) Providing negative feedback to a colleague on the quality of their work   face-to-face discussion

(4) A formal complaint to a supplier regarding the delivery times of goods, which are not as agreed   Letter

(5) Information to be provided to the sales director regarding the breakdown of sales geographically for the last two years Information to be provided to the sales director regarding the breakdown of sales geographically for the last two years   Email

Task 4.14

(a) The correct answer is:

	✓
Maintaining detailed customer records	
Preparing budgets and forecasts	✓
Sending out supplier statements	

(b) The correct answers are:

	✓
Spreadsheets are used to store and manipulate data.	✓
Spreadsheets can be used for word processing.	
Data in a spreadsheet can be easily updated.	✓
Spreadsheet data can be output in the form of graphs.	✓
Spreadsheets can be used to replace accounting packages.	
Sophisticated databases are making spreadsheets obsolete.	

Assessment objective 5 – Principles of bookkeeping controls

Task 5.1

The Journal

Account name	Amount £	Debit ✓	Credit ✓
Capital	4,780		✓
Office expenses	1,927	✓	
Sales	8,925		✓
Purchases	4,212	✓	
Commission received	75		✓
Discounts received	54		✓
Cash at bank	1,814	✓	
Petty cash	180	✓	
Bank loan	5,000		✓
Motor expenses	372	✓	
Motor vehicles	9,443	✓	
Other expenses	886	✓	

Journal to record opening entries of the new business.

Task 5.2

(a)

Account name	Amount £	Debit ✓	Credit ✓
Bank	12,565	✓	
Computer equipment	12,565		✓

(b)

Account name	Amount £	Debit ✓	Credit ✓
Computer equipment	12,265	✓	
Bank	12,265		✓

Task 5.3

(a) Commission received

 BPP

Details	Amount £	Details	Amount £
Rent received	545		

(b) Rent received

Details	Amount £	Details	Amount £
		Commission received	545

(c) Suspense

Details	Amount £	Details	Amount £
Balance b/f	2,682	General repairs	3,667
Legal fees	985		

(d) Legal fees

Details	Amount £	Details	Amount £
		Suspense	985

(e) General repairs

Details	Amount £	Details	Amount £
Suspense	3,667		

Task 5.4

Tutorial note. Cheque 001499 for £1,015 on the bank statement was taken into account in the previous bank reconciliation, since the difference between the opening balance on the bank statement and the cash book is £5,119 − £4,104 = £1,015. Therefore, it should not appear on the bank reconciliation.

Bank reconciliation statement as at 30 September 20XX	£
Balance as per bank statement	37,466
Add:	
Kington Ltd	3,970
Total to add	3,970
Less:	
Newton West	195
Welland Ltd	234
Roman plc	316

Bank reconciliation statement as at 30 September 20XX	£
Total to subtract	745
Balance as per cash book	40,691

Task 5.5

(a) Receivables ledger control account

Details	Amount £	Debit ✓	Credit ✓
Balance owing from credit customers at 1 July	101,912	✓	
Money received from credit customers	80,435		✓
Irrecoverable debts	228		✓
Goods sold to credit customers	70,419	✓	
Goods returned by credit customers	2,237		✓

(b) Payables ledger control account

Details	Amount £	Debit ✓	Credit ✓
Balance owing to credit suppliers at 1 July	61,926		✓
Journal debit to correct an error	550	✓	
Goods returned to credit suppliers	1,128	✓	
Purchases from credit suppliers	40,525		✓
Payments made to credit suppliers	45,763	✓	

(c) The correct answer is:

	✓
Credit balance b/d on 1 September of £65,050	
Debit balance b/d on 1 September of £65,050	✓
Credit balance b/d on 1 September of £67,500	
Debit balance b/d on 1 September of £67,500	

(d) The correct answers are:

Statements	True ✓	False ✓
The payables ledger control account enables a business to identify how much is owing to credit suppliers in total.	✓	

Statements	True ✓	False ✓
The total of the balances in the payables ledger should reconcile with the balance of the receivables ledger control account.		✓

Task 5.6

(a) VAT control

Details	Amount £	Details	Amount £
Balance b/f – owing from HMRC	13,146	Sales	31,197
Purchases	19,220	Purchases returns	2,465
Sales returns	1,779	Cash sales	1,910
Petty cash	98	VAT refund	7,131
Irrecoverable debts	950	Office equipment sold	200

(b) The correct answer is:

	✓
Yes	
No	✓

> **Tutorial note.** The balance is a £7,710 credit balance. That is the amount owed to HMRC.

(c) The correct answer is:

	✓
The VAT control account is used to record the VAT amount of transactions and to help prepare the VAT return.	✓
The VAT control account is used to record the VAT amount of transactions but has no connection with the VAT return.	

Task 5.7

(a)

Details	Amount £	Details	Amount £
Balance b/f	27,321	Sales returns	1,934
Sales	11,267	Bank	10,006
		Irrecoverable debts	742

Details	Amount £	Details	Amount £
		Balance c/d	25,906
	38,588		38,588

(b) Payables ledger control

Details	Amount £	Details	Amount £
Purchases returns	751	Balance b/f	6,547
Bank	8,653	Purchases	9,317
Discounts received	481		
Balance c/d	5,979		
	15,864		15,864

Task 5.8

(a)

	Control account ✓	List of balances ✓	Both ✓
Invoice entered into the sales day book as £540 instead of £450			✓
Purchases day book overcast by £1,100	✓		
An invoice taken as £430 instead of £330 when being posted to the customer's account		✓	
Incorrect balancing of a subsidiary ledger account		✓	
A purchases return not entered into the purchases returns day book			✓

(b) The correct answers are:

Transaction	Payment out ✓	Payment in ✓
£725 paid into the bank		✓
Direct debit of £47	✓	
Cheque payment of £124.60	✓	
Interest charged on the overdraft	✓	
BACS payment for wages	✓	

 BPP

ANSWERS

Task 5.9

(a) Receivables ledger control

Details	Amount £	Details	Amount £
Balance b/f	12,467	Sales returns	100
		Irrecoverable debts	250
		Balance c/d	12,117
	12,467		12,467
Balance c/d	12,117		

(b) Reconciliation

		£
Receivables ledger list of balances		11,858
Error	Over-statement of receipt (430 – 340)	90
Error	Balance omitted	169
Amended list of balances		12,117
Amended control account balance		12,117

Task 5.10

(a)

Account name	Amount £	Debit ✓	Credit ✓
Wages expense	23,648	✓	
Wages control	23,648		✓

Working

£21,999 + £1,649 = £23,648

(b)

Account name	Amount £	Debit ✓	Credit ✓
Wages control	14,018	✓	
Bank	14,018		✓

Working

£21,999 – £5,755 – £1,476 – £750

(c) The correct answer is:

	✓
Recording a bank payment for office expenses on the debit side of the office furniture account.	
Recording a payment for motor expenses in the bank account, the motor expenses account and the miscellaneous expenses account. (Ignore VAT)	
Recording a payment by cheque to a credit supplier in the bank account and payables ledger control account only.	
Recording a cash payment for travel expenses in the cash account only. (Ignore VAT)	✓

Assessment objective 6 – The business environment

Task 6.1

(a) The correct answers are:

Statement	True ✓	False ✓
Charna Ltd will have to pay damages to Larma Ltd even though it notified the company before the delivery date.	✓	
Charna Ltd has committed anticipatory breach of contract.	✓	
Larma Ltd must continue to perform its obligations and deliver the furniture in May.		✓

Charna Ltd has committed anticipatory breach of contract. This occurs when a party declares that they will break the terms of the contract before the time for performance has arrived.

Due to Charna Ltd's breach of contract, Larma Ltd may treat the contract as discharged and is not required to perform its obligations under it. The breach of contract allows Larma Ltd to recover damages for any losses it has incurred.

(b) The correct answers are:

Statement	True ✓	False ✓
In a criminal case, the state is the prosecutor.	✓	
In a criminal case, the prosecutor must prove their case on the balance of probability.		✓
In a civil case, the burden of proof is on the defendant.		✓
In a civil case, there is no concept of punishment.	✓	

In a criminal case, the State is the prosecutor (because the community as a whole suffers as a result of the law being broken) who brings the case against the accused. The prosecutor must prove its case beyond reasonable doubt.

In a civil case, the burden of proof rests with the claimant and there is no concept of punishment. Compensation is paid to the wronged person.

(c) The correct answers are:

Statement	Second reading ✓	Report stage ✓
Debate on the general merits of the Bill. No amendments at this stage.	✓	
The Bill as amended in committee is reported to the full House for approval.		✓

Both statements define what happens at each stage.

Task 6.2

(a) The correct answers are:

Statement	True ✓	False ✓
Liquidated damages are a genuine pre-estimate of losses that are written into the terms of a contract.	✓	
Penalty clauses are an alternative to liquidated damages which courts enforce to punish those in breach on contract.		✓

Liquidated damages are a genuine pre-estimate of losses that are written into the terms of the contract. They are generally permitted by the courts. Penalty clauses are designed to punish the party in breach of contract and courts generally will not allow them.

(b) The correct answers are:

Statement	Correct ✓	Incorrect ✓
Executed consideration is a promise given in return for a promise		✓
Consideration must be in the form of money to be valid		✓

Executed consideration is consideration provided at the time the contract is made and is an act done in return for a promise. Executory consideration is a promise to do something in the future.

Consideration can be in the form of money, goods or services.

(c) The correct answers are:

Statement	True ✓	False ✓
Acceptance of an offer must be in the form of spoken or written words.		✓
Acceptance may not be made by silence.	✓	
Under the postal rule, acceptance is completed when the letter is delivered to the offeror.		✓
If acceptance is sent by email, then acceptance is completed when the email is sent.		✓

Silence does not constitute acceptance; there must be some form of indication of assent to the offer, orally in writing or by deed.

Under the postal rule, acceptance is completed when the letter is posted. This rule does not apply to email. Acceptance by email is only completed when it is received by the offeror.

Task 6.3

(a) The correct answers are:

Statement	True ✓	False ✓
Intention is not presumed where two spouses are separating.		✓
Intention is presumed in commercial agreements.	✓	

Intention is not normally presumed in domestic situations, however where spouses are separating is an exception.

Intention is presumed in commercial agreements.

(b) The correct answers are:

Circumstance	Offer terminated ✓	Offer not terminated ✓
The offeree sends a counter offer	✓	
A reasonable time has passed since the offer was made	✓	
There is a failure of a condition of the offer	✓	

These are all circumstances where an offer will be terminated. Others include: express rejection, revocation and death of the offeror and offeree.

Task 6.4

(a) The correct answers are:

Statement	Expectation interest ✓	Reliance interest ✓
The amount awarded as damages is what is needed to compensate the injured party for wasted expenditure due to performing on the contract.		✓
The amount awarded as damages is what is needed to put the claimant in the position they would have achieved if the contract had been performed.	✓	

Damages to protect a claimant's expectation interest is what is needed to put them in the position they would have achieved if the contract had been performed.

A claimant may alternatively seek to have their reliance interest protected. This refers to the position they would have been in had they not relied on the contract. For example, it would compensate for wasted expenditure due to relying on the contract.

 BPP

(b) The correct answers are:

Statement	Void contract ✓	Voidable contract ✓	Unenforceable contract ✓
The contract is valid but performance by one party cannot be enforced			✓
There is no contract	✓		
The innocent party can withdraw from the contract		✓	

The statements define each type of contract.

(c)

Statement	Rectification ✓	Rescission ✓	Injunction ✓	Specific performance ✓
Restoration of the pre-contract status quo		✓		
The defendant must do what they had agreed to do				✓
The alteration of a document to reflect the parties' true intentions	✓			
The defendant must abstain from wrongdoing			✓	

The statements define each type of remedy.

Task 6.5

(a) The correct answers are:

Statement	Correct ✓	Incorrect ✓
The Act only applies to exclusion clauses.		✓
A business may be classified as acting as a consumer in some contracts.	✓	
Under the Act, some terms are deemed to be automatically enforceable.		✓

The Consumer Rights Act 20015 applies to all unfair terms in contracts, not just unfair exclusion clauses. A business may be classified as a consumer if the contract is incidental to its main business.

Under the Act, some terms are deemed to be automatically unenforceable, not automatically enforceable.

(b) The correct answers are:

Statement	Correct ✓	Incorrect ✓
Damages are a common law remedy.	✓	
Damages are generally only payable for economic losses.	✓	
Equitable remedies are only awarded at the discretion of the court.	✓	

Damages are a common law, not an equitable remedy. They are the usual remedy granted for breach of contract and are used to compensate for economic (financial) losses.

Equitable remedies are awarded at the discretion of the court and are not automatically granted on request by the claimant.

(c) The correct answers are:

Statement	Small claims track ✓	Multi-track ✓	Fast track ✓
Hears cases with a value of over £25,000		✓	
Hears cases with a value of between £10,000 and £25,000			✓
Hears cases with a value of under £10,000	✓		

The small claims track deals with uncomplicated claims with a value under £10,000 in the County Court.

The fast track deals with cases with a value between £10,000 and £25,000 that will last for a day or less. Cases are heard at the Country Court.

Multi-track cases have a value of over £25,000 or are complex, and are heard at the High Court.

(d)

Court	1st ✓	2nd ✓	3rd ✓	4th ✓	5th ✓
Crown court				✓	
Supreme court	✓				
Magistrate's court					✓
Court of Appeal		✓			
High court			✓		

Hierarchy of criminal law courts
Supreme Court Final appeal court
Court of Appeal Hears appeals from Crown Courts.
High Court Hears some appeals from Magistrate's and Crown Courts.
Crown Court Tries major offences and hears appeals from Magistrate's Courts for minor offences.
Magistrate's Court Tries minor offences, passes major offences to the Crown Court.

BPP

Assessment objective 7 – The business environment/Introduction to bookkeeping/Principles of Bookkeeping Controls

Task 7.1

(a) The correct answer is:

	✓
1 year	
3 years	
6 years	✓
9 years	

Banking records should be kept for six years.

(b) The correct answers are:

Statement	Data analytics ✓	Distributed ledger technology ✓
Technology that allows organisations and individuals who are unconnected to share an agreed record of events, such as ownership of an asset.		✓
The collection, management and analysis of large data sets (such as big data) with the objective of discovering useful information such as customer buying patterns, that an organisation can use for decision making.	✓	

The statements describe each type of technology.

(c) Any three from the following:

- Breaches of confidentiality (as employees can access all information on the computer)
- Breaches of data protection legislation (due to lack of robust security of data)
- Access to information (including personal files)
- Potential theft or fraud (as employees may have access to the business bank account)
- Hacking and other cybersecurity risks (due to insecure password)

Task 7.2

(a) In a manual system, the sale is recorded in a sales day book. This sales-day book is totalled and the total is transferred to the receivables ledger control account. Every individual transaction is recorded in the individual customer account in the receivables ledger.

The same process is used to record payments from customers and credit notes issued for returns (recorded in sales day book which is totaled and the total recorded in the receivables ledger control account). Individual transactions are then recorded in the individual customer accounts in the receivables ledger.

At the end of each period, the receivables ledger is totaled and checked to the receivables ledger control account total. Any errors are identified and corrected.

In a digital system, a sale is recorded. The sale is automatically posted to the receivables ledger control account and the individual customer account. In consequence, there are no differences between the ledger and control. Both are automatically reconciled.

Only entering the transaction once means considerable time is saved and errors reduced.

(b) The correct answer is:

	✓
Comparable	
Understandable	✓
Consistent	
Relevant and reliable	

Understandable information is presented in a clear format and in easy-to-read language that allows readers to fully appreciate the information that is being presented.

(c) The correct answer is:

	✓
Volume	
Velocity	
Value	
Variety	
Veracity	✓

Veracity concerns the trustworthiness or accuracy of big data. Despite an organisation's best efforts, data sets will contain inaccuracies, bias, anomalies and 'noise'. Therefore, as much as possible needs to be done to clean up the data before it can be trusted as accurate.

Task 7.3

(a) The correct answer is:

	✓
Comparable	
Understandable	
Consistent	✓
Relevant and reliable	

Using the same methods and policies each time describes consistency.

(b) Any three from:

- Financial loss
- Damage to reputation
- Loss of faith by customers
- Disruption to the organisation

 BPP

ANSWERS

(c) The correct answer is:

	✓
Pharming	
Hacking	
Phishing	✓
Keylogging	

In a phishing attack, the cyberattacker sends emails to the victim which appear to be from a trusted source, for example a bank. The emails request the victim sends back security information (such as usernames and passwords) and personal details and uses them to steal funds from the victim.

Task 7.4

(a) The correct answer is:

	✓
1 year after leaving employment	
3 years in total	
6 years in total	✓
9 years in total	

Employee records should be kept for six years in total.

(b) The correct answer is:

	✓
Processed data	
Open data	
Machine generated data	
Human-sourced data	✓

Big data originates from several sources:

- Processed data – originating from existing databases of business and other organisations

- Open data – originating from the public sector data (for example, transport, Government financial and public service data)

- Human-sourced data – originating from social networks, blogs, emails, text messages and internet searches

- Machine-generated data – originating from fixed and mobile sensors, as well as computer and website logs

(c) Any three from the following:

- The non-removal of data and equipment from the premises

- The frequent backing-up of computerised data, and the storage of backups separately from the original data, so that there are safe copies in case of systems failure, data corruption or fire
- The use of anti-virus software, firewalls and other protective tools on all computers, to prevent malicious corruption and theft of data
- The use of passwords to restrict access to computer systems or files (often with additional policies regarding the complexity and regular change of passwords) to prevent unauthorised users from obtaining, amending or deleting them
- The use of authorisations to control access to security-coded paper-based files
- The non-divulging of passwords, security codes and other data security measures to other parties

Task 7.5

(a) In a manual system, the purchase is recorded in a purchases day book. This purchases day book is totalled and the total is transferred to the payables ledger control account. Every individual transaction is recorded in the individual supplier account in the payables ledger.

The same process is used to record payments to suppliers and credit notes for returns (recorded in purchases day book which is totalled and the total recorded in the payables ledger control account). Individual transactions are then recorded in the individual supplier accounts in the payables ledger.

At the end of each period, the payables ledger is totalled and checked to the payables ledger control account total. Any errors are identified and corrected.

In a digital system, a purchase is recorded. The purchase is automatically posted to the payables ledger control account and the individual supplier account. In consequence, there are no differences between the ledger and control. Both are automatically reconciled.

Only entering the transaction once means considerable time is saved and errors reduced.

(b) The correct answer is:

Relevant and reliable	
Understandable	
Comparable	
Timely	✓

Timely information is made available when needed (before or at the time of the decision).

(c) The correct answer is:

Access control	
Malware and virus protection	
Boundary firewalls and internet gateways	✓
Secure configuration	

Firewalls and internet gateways are software protections that intercept data being transmitted in and out of a system.

 BPP

Task 7.6

(a)

Department to which the accounting department will provide information	Information
Sales department	Analysis of sales revenue by region compared to budget
Purchasing department	Discrepancies between supplier invoices and purchase orders

(b) For the accountant, automation and artificial intelligence (AI) can help in the recording of transactions in financial systems. Accounting software can automatically download transactions from an organisation's online bank account. Once this has been done, the system's artificial intelligence can assign transactions to appropriate nominal codes and record the transactions appropriately in the accounts. This intelligence is achieved by the user recording the transactions manually a few times before the system learns what types of transactions should be assigned to which nominal codes.

For the auditor, systems are available that perform complete checks on financial data held, allowing 100% of transactions to be audited automatically on a continuous basis, removing the need for an auditor to perform routine audit checks to verify transactions.

(c) The correct answer is:

	✓
Distributed denial of service (DDoS) attack	✓
Keylogging	
Screenshot manager	
Ad clicker	

In a distributed denial of service attack (DDoS), the cyberattacker attempts to disrupt an organisation's online activities by preventing people from accessing the organisation's website. Botnets (large numbers of individual computers which have been taken over without the user knowing) are instructed to overwhelm the organisation's website with a wave of internet traffic so that the system is unable to handle it and may cause it to crash.

 BPP

Assessment objective 8 – The business environment

Task 8.1

(a) The correct answers are:

Statement	True ✓	False ✓
Risk is the chance of damage being done to an organisation.	✓	
Businesses cannot avoid uncertainty.	✓	

Uncertainty is created where a business cannot measure or foresee an event or situation occurring. It is unavoidable in business life.

Risk is the chance of an event occurring that causes loss or damage to a business.

(b) The correct answers are:

Tax	Revenue ✓	Capital ✓
Corporation tax	✓	
Inheritance tax		✓
National insurance	✓	

Income tax is another revenue tax. Capital gains tax, as its name suggests, is another capital tax.

(c) The correct answers are:

Statement	Micro-economics ✓	Macro-economics ✓
Determines how much of a good consumers will buy at a particular price	✓	
Concerned with issues such as taxation and interest rates		✓
Relates to a specific country		✓

Micro-economics describes the forces of supply and demand within individual markets. Macro-economics describes the wider economy that all businesses and industries operate in within a particular country.

Task 8.2

(a) The correct answer is:

	✓
The value of money rises as inflation rises	
Inflation does not impact on the value of money	
The value of money will fall as inflation rises	✓

 BPP

Inflation is where there is a rise in prices generally. This means the value of money falls.

(b) The correct answer is:

	✓
Economy	
Fairness	✓
Equity	

Economy is the principle that the tax system should not cost an excessive amount.

The principle of fairness says that the right amount of tax should be generated at the right time. The tax system should be designed to prevent instances of double taxation and accidental non-taxation.

Equity concerns the burden of tax faced by taxpayers.

(c) The correct answers are:

Statement	True ✓	False ✓
The equilibrium price for a market is always fixed.		✓
The equilibrium price is the lowest price charged for a good in the market.		✓
The equilibrium price is the price of a good where the volume demanded and the volume supplied in a market are the same.	✓	

The equilibrium price is the price of a good where the volume demanded by customers and the volume supplied by businesses are the same. It is not the average price charged for a good.

An equilibrium price is not fixed, but will change as the demand and supply curves shift.

Task 8.3

(a) The correct answers are:

	✓
Government spending	
Interest rates	✓
Exchange rates	✓
Taxation	

The other instrument of monetary policy is reserve requirements.

Tax and Government spending are instruments of fiscal policy.

 BPP

(b) The correct answer is:

	✓
Luxury	
Inferior	✓
Normal	

Demand for an inferior good will fall as consumer incomes rise.

The opposite is true for normal and luxury goods.

(c) The correct answer is:

	✓
Every business organisation is motivated by profit	
Making short-term losses is consistent with the profit motive	✓
The profit motive describes the purpose of organisations to make the local economy wealthier	

Making the business's owners wealthier is the main motivation for profit-seeking organisations.

Not all businesses are motivated by profit (eg, not-for-profit organisations).

Even though organisations are motivated by making a profit, some might be willing in the short-term to break-even or even make small losses if it means that their market position is strengthened so they can earn larger profits in the future.

Task 8.4

(a) The correct answers are:

	Benefit ✓	Disadvantage ✓
Government incentives	✓	
Market size	✓	
Logistics		✓

Trading globally means that organisations may be able to take advantage of Government incentives to invest. It also means an increased number of buyers in the global market.

Globally trading businesses often have problems in logistics, such as distributing goods and facilitating customer returns.

(b) The correct answer is:

	✓
Price	
Population	
Political	✓

The other PESTEL factors are Economic, Social, Environmental and Legal.

 BPP

(c) The correct answers are:

Tax	Direct ✓	Indirect ✓
Capital gains tax	✓	
VAT		✓
Inheritance tax	✓	

In the UK, most taxes are direct, but VAT is an exception.

Task 8.5

(a) The correct answers are:

Factor	Affects demand ✓	Affects supply ✓
Production costs		✓
Interrelated goods	✓	
Income levels	✓	

Consumer income will impact on how much of a good will be demanded. Demand can increase or even fall depending on the type of good, such as inter-related goods (substitutes and complements).

Production costs will impact supply. If they are too high, suppliers may be put off producing them, especially if the price they sell for is not attractive.

(b) The correct answer is:

	✓
Where there is deflation, the value of money will rise.	✓
Deflation does not affect the value of money.	
Where there is deflation, the value of money will fall.	

Deflation is where there is a fall in prices generally. This means the value of money rises.

(c) The correct answers are:

	✓
Reserve requirements	
Government spending	✓
Interest rates	
Taxation	✓

Fiscal policy involves taxation and Government spending. Interest and exchange rates plus reserve requirements are instruments of monetary policy.

ANSWERS

AAT Q2022
Practice Assessments

Level 2 Synoptic Assessment

You are advised to attempt practice assessments online from the AAT website. This will ensure you are prepared for how the assessment will be presented on the AAT's system when you attempt the real assessment. Please access the assessment using the address below:

https://www.aat.org.uk/training/study-support/search

The AAT may call the assessments on their website, under study support resources, either a 'practice assessment' or 'sample assessment'.

BPP Practice Assessment 1

Level 2 Synoptic Assessment

Time allowed: 2 hours

Level 2 Synoptic Assessment

BPP Practice Assessment 1

Assessment information

You have **2 hours** to complete this practice assessment.

- This assessment contains **8 tasks** and you should attempt to complete **every** task.
- Each task is independent. You will not need to refer to your answers to previous tasks.
- The total number of marks for this assessment is **100**.
- Read every task carefully to make sure you understand what is required.
- Where the date is relevant, it is given in the task data.
- Both minus signs and brackets can be used to indicate negative numbers, **unless** task instructions state otherwise.
- You must use a full stop to indicate a decimal point. For example, write 100.57 **not** 100,57 or 10057.
- You may use a comma to indicate a number in the thousands, but you don't have to. For example, 10000 and 10,000 are both acceptable.

Task 1 (10 marks)

This task is about different business types and their functions.

Required

(a) Identify whether the following statements regarding entities and the entity concept are true or false.

	True ✓	False ✓
The entity concept means that the owners of the business can be separate from those who manage it.		
All business entities have limited liability.		
The accounts of business entities must not reflect the financial position of the owners.		

(3 marks)

Your sister and her partner are thinking of setting up a business organisation and would like some advice on which type of legal structure they should go for.

Required

(b) Identify whether the followings statements about legal structures for businesses are true or false

	True ✓	False ✓
Your sister and her partner are prevented in law from setting up as a partnership.		
Setting up a business as a company limited by guarantee means neither your sister nor her partner would have to contribute any capital unless the company is wound up.		
If your sister and her partner wish to raise finance in the future by selling shares, they can only do this if they set up a public limited company.		

(3 marks)

(c) All of the following documents must be submitted to the Registrar of Companies to form a company except one. Which is the exception?

	✓
Memorandum of association	
Articles of association	
Statement of compliance	

(1 mark)

(d) Which function plans, organises, directs and controls the activities to provide products and services?

	✓
Finance	
Operations	
Marketing	

(1 mark)

(e) Which function determines which products and services should be produced?

	✓
Marketing	
Finance	
Operations	

(1 mark)

(f) Which function moves raw materials from storage to where they are needed for production?

	✓
Operations	
Information technology	
Logistics	

(1 mark)

Task 2 (13 marks)

This task is about the finance function, its information requirements, and its role within the wider organisation.

You have recently received a promotion to assistant accountant to reflect the fact that you have nearly completed your AAT training. The finance manager has asked you to prepare some information about the finance function to help new starters in the team.

Required

(a) Which of the following parties is responsible for a business' costing analysis?

	✓
The directors	
The shareholders	
The internal auditors	
The management accountants	

(1 mark)

 BPP

(b) Which of the following parties is responsible for preparing an audit report which states that the statutory financial statements show a true and fair view of the financial position of the company?

	✓
The finance director	
The financial accountants	
The external auditor	
The board of directors	

(1 mark)

(c) Which of the following groups requires customer account balances?

	✓
Operations function	
Sales and marketing function	
Human resources function	

(1 mark)

(d) Which of the following groups requires information on bonus payments due to employees?

	✓
HMRC	
Payroll function	
HR	

(1 mark)

(e) Identify which business function would be interested in the following information from the finance function.

Information supplied	Sales and marketing ✓	Logistics ✓
Average delivery times to customers		
Revenue generated per product type		
Storage costs for raw materials		

(3 marks)

A fellow AAT student at your workplace is having problems prioritising his work. He has been asked to prepare a finance report for a meeting of department heads which is at 12.00pm today. The report will take one hour and is in addition to his routine daily tasks which are as follows:

Task	Time needed for task	Description
Processing expense claims	1 hour	Must be completed at the start of the day
Dealing with emails sent to finance team	1 hour	Must be completed during the working day
Reviewing purchase invoices	1 hour	Daily task that must be completed by the end of the working day
Setting up payment run	1 hour	Must be completed after review of purchase invoices
Lunch break	1 hour	Must be taken between 12pm–1pm
Cover finance team phone line	2 × 1 hour	One hour in the morning and one hour in the afternoon

Required

(f) **(i)** **Which of the following tasks should be done between 9am-10am?**

	✓
Prepare finance report for the meeting	
Dealing with emails sent to finance team	
Processing expense claims	

(1 mark)

(ii) **Which of the following tasks should be done between 10am-11am?**

	✓
Prepare finance report for the meeting	
Reviewing purchase invoices	
Cover finance team phone line	

(1 mark)

(iii) **Which of the following tasks should be done between 11am–12pm?**

	✓
Setting up payment run	
Prepare finance report for the meeting	
Cover finance team phone line	

(1 mark)

You work in the finance department and have been told that a colleague who works on your company's front desk at lunchtime has had to take some time off over the next few days due to illness. You manager has asked you to cover for her even though this is something not included in your job description.

 BPP

Required

(g) Identify the type of task you have been asked to perform.

	✓
Routine	
Urgent	
Unexpected	

(1 mark)

(h) Identify whether the following statements about information are true or false.

Statement	True ✓	False ✓
An advantage of primary information is that the investigator knows where the information has come from.		
A disadvantage of primary information is that the investigator may not be aware of any inadequacies or limitations in the information.		

(2 marks)

Task 3 (14 marks)

This task is about corporate social responsibility (CSR), ethics and sustainability.

Required

(a) Identify which of the following statements about business ethics are true or false.

Statement	True ✓	False ✓
Businesses are not morally responsible for their actions.		
A business's ethics may be found in its culture.		
Ethical values may be taught in employee training programmes.		

(3 marks)

(b) Identify the stakeholder from the statement using the picklist and identify whether they are internal or external stakeholders.

Statement	Stakeholder	Internal ✓	External ✓
These stakeholders expect products sold to have good quality.	▼		
These stakeholders expect interest to be paid to them.	▼		

Picklist

- Customers
- Government
- Lenders
- Local community
- Managers
- Suppliers

(4 marks)

The AAT *Code of Professional Ethics* for accounting technicians includes five fundamental principles.

Required

(c) Which TWO of the following statements relate to the principle of integrity?

	✓
To be straightforward	
To avoid bias	
To comply with relevant laws	
To be honest	

(2 marks)

You are visiting an old friend who happens to be an employee of a client that you are externally auditing. She has heard rumours that the company could be taken over by a competitor in the near future and is concerned about her job. You have heard the rumours as well and know that, despite take-over talks having taken place, the interested buyer has decided not to proceed and, therefore, your friend's job is safe. The two of you are alone at your friend's house when she asks you if you have any news about the take-over.

Required

(d) Identify which of the following statements concerning the situation are true or false.

Statement	True ✓	False ✓
There is a threat to professional behaviour.		
Professional ethics extend to your personal life.		
Because no one else will hear, you are permitted to tell her that the take-over is not going ahead.		

(3 marks)

Lucy is a newly qualified member of AAT and is keen to ensure that she follows the AAT *Code of Professional Ethics* at all times. Working in practice, Lucy knows of the importance of demonstrating her objectivity to her clients.

Required

(e) Identify TWO actions that Lucy could take to demonstrate her objectivity.

	✓
Avoiding personal relationships with clients	
Complying with her firm's data protection policy	
Keeping her mind clear of prejudice and bias	
Behaving in a manner that does not discredit the profession	

(2 marks)

Task 4 (22 marks)

This task is about processing bookkeeping transactions and communicating information.

You are working as an accounts clerk at Holmbush Designs Ltd and report to your supervisor, Jack Sterling.

The following credit transactions have been entered into the sales returns day book as shown below. No entries have yet been made into the ledgers.

Sales returns day book

Date	Details	Credit note number	Total	VAT	Net
20XX			£	£	£
30 Jun	Wem Designs	CN221	1,128	188	940
30 Jun	Bailey and Byng	CN222	354	59	295
	Totals		1,482	247	1,235

Required

(a) What will be the entries in the receivables ledger?

Receivables ledger

Account name	Amount £	Debit ✓	Credit ✓
▼			
▼			

Picklist
- Bailey and Byng
- Payables ledger control
- Purchases
- Purchases returns
- Receivables ledger control
- Sales
- Sales returns
- VAT

- Wem Designs

(4 marks)

(b) What will be the entries in the general ledger?

General ledger

Account name	Amount £	Debit ✓	Credit ✓
▼			
▼			
▼			

Picklist

- Bailey and Byng
- Payables ledger control
- Purchases
- Purchases returns
- Receivables ledger control
- Sales
- Sales returns
- VAT
- Wem Designs

(6 marks)

Jack has been asked by the finance director to look into the possibility of introducing cloud computing at Holmbush Designs Ltd.

Required

(c) State the difference between a public and private cloud. (2 marks)

 BPP

You are now required to respond to the email below which you have just received from Jack Sterling.

From:	Jacksterling@ABC.com
To:	Accountingtechnician@ABC.com
Cc:	
Subject:	Purpose of the journal and its entries
Date:	01/08/20XX

Hello (your name),

Thank you for completing the journal entry task this morning.

Jessica Khan, the owner of the business, has sent me an email asking for an explanation of the purpose of a journal, and the types of entries that can be recorded.

I am in meetings this afternoon, so could you please respond to Jessica on my behalf? Jessica has mentioned that she would like to receive a response by the end of today.

I would be grateful if you would copy me into your reply.

Jessica's email address is: Khancatering@info.com

Many thanks,

Regards,

Jack

Jack Sterling

Office Supervisor

Required

(d) In accordance with your supervisor's instructions, prepare an email to be sent to Jessica Khan.

From: Accountingtechnician@ABC.com

To:

Cc:

Subject:

Date:

(10 marks)

Task 5 (10 marks)

This task is about control accounts, reconciliations and using journals to correct accounts.

You are employed at Benswick Ltd as an accounts clerk. You work on both receivables and payables.

The following is a summary of transactions with credit customers during the month of July.

Required

(a) Show whether each entry will be a debit or credit in the receivables ledger control account in the general ledger.

Receivables ledger control account

Details	Amount £	Debit ✓	Credit ✓
Balance owing from credit customers at 1 July	101,912		
Money received from credit customers	80,435		
Irrecoverable debts	228		
Goods sold to credit customers	70,419		

(4 marks)

 BPP

The following is a summary of transactions with credit suppliers during the month of July.

Required

(b) Show whether each entry will be a debit or credit in the payables ledger control account in the general ledger.

Payables ledger control account

Details	Amount £	Debit ✓	Credit ✓
Balance owing to credit suppliers at 1 July	61,926		
Payment made to credit suppliers	550		
Goods returned to credit suppliers	1,128		

(3 marks)

At the beginning of September, the following balances were in the receivables ledger.

	Balances	
Credit customers	Amount £	Debit/Credit
CTC Ltd	11,122	Debit
J B Estates	8,445	Debit
Koo Designs	23,119	Debit
PJB Ltd	1,225	Credit
Probyn pic	19,287	Debit
Yen Products	4,302	Debit

Required

(c) What should be the balance of the receivables ledger control account in order for it to reconcile with the total of the balances in the receivables ledger?

	✓
Credit balance b/d on 1 September of £65,050	
Debit balance b/d on 1 September of £65,050	
Credit balance b/d on 1 September of £67,500	
Debit balance b/d on 1 September of £67,500	

(1 mark)

(d) Show whether each of the following statements is true or false.

Statements	True ✓	False ✓
The payables ledger control account enables a business to identify how much is owing to credit suppliers in total.		
The total of the balances in the payables ledger should reconcile with the balance of the receivables ledger control account.		

(2 marks)

Task 6 (7 marks)

This task is about the principles of contract law.

Required

(a) **Identify whether the following statements regarding consideration are correct or incorrect.**

Statement	Correct ✓	Incorrect ✓
Consideration does not have to be sufficient or adequate.		
Except where the parties gain a mutual benefit, the performance of existing contractual obligations is not sufficient to support a promise of additional reward.		
Executory consideration is a promise to perform an action.		

(3 marks)

(b) **Match the following statements to the stage in the process of creating legislation.**

Statement	First reading ✓	Committee stage ✓
The bill is introduced and added to Parliament's agenda.		
The bill is considered by specialists.		

(2 marks)

(c) **Identify whether the following statements regarding breach of contract are true or false.**

Statement	True ✓	False ✓
Only reasonably foreseeable losses suffered by an injured party due to breach of contract can be recovered in damages.		
Penalty clauses are a genuine pre-estimate of losses that are written into the terms of a contract.		

(2 marks)

 BPP

Task 7 (10 marks)

This task is about bookkeeping systems, receipts and payments, and the importance of information and data security.

Luka is the owner of a small business that buys and sells expensive rugs. He has three employees who perform a range of roles. Only Luka has access to a business computer, but he very often gives his password to employees so they can check emails and perform admin work while he is not around.

Required

(a) State THREE business risks associated with Luka's computer security.   (3 marks)

Luka is very careful to analyse his business' financial performance every year. When doing so, he always uses the same methods and policies to calculate his figures.

Required

(b) Which characteristic of useful information does Luka apply?

	✓
Comparable	
Understandable	
Consistent	
Relevant and reliable	

(1 mark)

(c) How long should Luka keep employee records for?

	✓
Until the employee leaves	
3 years	
6 years	
9 years	

(1 mark)

Luka is thinking of introducing a cloud-based accounting system that records business transactions digitally. Previously, he operated a manual system for recording business transactions.

Required

(d) Using the example of a purchase from a supplier, explain how the two systems for recording transactions differ.

Your answer should refer to the books of prime entry, the payables ledger and the payables ledger control account.   (5 marks)

Task 8 (14 marks)

This task is about the external business environment.

Matterface Ltd produces a single product. Demand for the product falls when consumer incomes rise.

Required

(a) Which of the following types of good does Matterface Ltd produce?

	✓
Giffen	
Inferior	
Substitute	

(1 mark)

(b) Identify whether the following statements regarding uncertainty and risk are true or false.

Statement	True ✓	False ✓
Businesses cannot avoid risk entirely.		
Businesses can avoid uncertainty.		
Insurance is a method of mitigating risk.		

(3 marks)

(c) Which of the following statements is correct regarding deflation?

	✓
The value of money will fall	
The value of money rises	
There is no change in the value of money	

(1 mark)

(d) Identify whether the following are benefits or disadvantages to a business of trading globally.

	Benefit ✓	Disadvantage ✓
Access to resources		
Cultural differences		
Market size		

(3 marks)

(e) Which of the following principles of an effective tax system is related to the burden of tax faced by taxpayers?

	✓
Economy	
Fairness	
Equity	

(1 mark)

(f) Identify whether the following taxes are revenue or capital taxes.

Tax	Revenue ✓	Capital ✓
Income tax		
Corporation tax		
Inheritance tax		

(3 marks)

(g) Identify TWO instruments of monetary policy.

	✓
Reserve requirements	
Taxation	
Government spending	
Interest rates	

(2 marks)

BPP Practice Assessment 1

Level 2 Synoptic Assessment

Answers

Task 1

(a) The correct answers are:

	True ✓	False ✓
The entity concept means that the owners of the business can be separate from those who manage it.	✓	
All business entities have limited liability.		✓
The accounts of business entities must not reflect the financial position of the owners.	✓	

The entity concept allows the separation of business ownership from management. Accounts of business entities should only reflect the performance and financial position of the business.

Not all business entities have limited liability (for example, traditional partnerships).

(b) The correct answers are:

	True ✓	False ✓
Your sister and her partner are prevented in law from setting up as a partnership.		✓
Setting up a business as a company limited by guarantee means neither your sister nor her partner would have to contribute any capital unless the company is wound up.	✓	
If your sister and her partner wish to raise finance in the future by selling shares, they can only do this if they set up a public limited company.		✓

There is nothing in law preventing your sister and her partner from setting up as a partnership.

Companies limited by guarantee do not have share capital and the members only have to contribute what they have guaranteed in the event of a winding up.

Private companies can also raise finance by selling shares; they just cannot sell the shares publicly.

(c) The correct answer is:

	✓
Memorandum of association	
Articles of association	✓
Statement of compliance	

If the Articles of association are not submitted to the Registrar, then the company will be formed with model articles.

 BPP

ANSWERS

(d) The correct answer is:

	✓
Finance	
Operations	✓
Marketing	

(e) The correct answer is:

	✓
Marketing	✓
Finance	
Operations	

(f) The correct answer is:

	✓
Operations	
Information technology	
Logistics	✓

Task 2

(a) The correct answer is:

	✓
The directors	
The shareholders	
The internal auditors	
The management accountants	✓

(b) The correct answer is:

	✓
The finance director	
The financial accountants	
The external auditor	✓
The board of directors	

The management accountants are responsible for providing costing information. The external auditor states whether the financial statements show a true and fair view.

(c) The correct answer is:

	✓
Operations function	
Sales and marketing function	✓
Human resources function	

(d) The correct answer is:

	✓
HMRC	
Payroll function	✓
HR	

Sales and marketing need a customer's account balance to help them decide whether to sell them more products or not.

Payroll needs details of bonus payments due so they can process them and pay the employees the correct amount.

(e) The correct answers are:

Information supplied	Sales and marketing ✓	Logistics ✓
Average delivery times to customers		✓
Revenue generated per product type	✓	
Storage costs for raw materials		✓

Logistics are responsible for storing and moving materials and finished goods. Therefore, information on delivery times and storage costs should be sent there. Revenue per product type is relevant to sales and marketing which needs to ensure products sold are profitable.

(f) (i) The correct answer is:

	✓
Prepare finance report for the meeting	
Dealing with emails sent to finance team	
Processing expense claims	✓

(ii) The correct answer is:

	✓
Prepare finance report for the meeting	✓
Reviewing purchase invoices	
Cover finance team phone line	

(iii) The correct answer is:

	✓
Setting up payment run	
Prepare finance report for the meeting	
Cover finance team phone line	✓

Processing expense claims must be completed at the start of the day, making it the first priority. The next priority is preparing finance report for the meeting. It is better to start this task as early as possible in case something happens to delay you. The only other task that must be performed in the morning is covering the finance team phone line.

Reviewing the purchase invoices and setting up the payment run are daily tasks that can be done in the afternoon.

(g) The correct answer is:

	✓
Routine	
Urgent	
Unexpected	✓

The task is not routine because it is not included in your job description. It is not urgent because there is no deadline that needs to be met. It is unexpected because it falls outside of your routine tasks.

(h) The correct answers are:

Statement	True ✓	False ✓
An advantage of primary information is that the investigator knows where the information has come from.	✓	
A disadvantage of primary information is that the investigator may not be aware of any inadequacies or limitations in the information.		✓

Primary information is collected by the investigator themselves. Therefore, they know where it has come from as well as any inadequacies or limitations of it.

Task 3

(a) The correct answers are:

Statement	True ✓	False ✓
Businesses are not morally responsible for their actions.		✓
A business's ethics may be found in its culture.	✓	
Ethical values may be taught in employee training programmes.	✓	

The concept of business ethics suggests that businesses are morally responsible for their actions.

Business ethics can be taught in employee training programmes and found in a business's culture

(b)

Statement	Stakeholder	Internal ✓	External ✓
These stakeholders expect products sold to have good quality.	Customers		✓
These stakeholders expect interest to be paid to them.	Lenders		✓

Customers expect products sold to them to be good quality. Lenders expect interest to be paid to them as a return on their investment. Both are external to a business.

(c) The correct answers are:

	✓
To be straightforward	✓
To avoid bias	
To comply with relevant laws	
To be honest	✓

The principle of integrity states that a member shall be 'straightforward and honest in all professional and business relationships'.

Avoiding bias is part of the principle of objectivity.

Complying with relevant laws and regulations is part of the principle of professional behaviour.

(d) The correct answers are:

Statement	True ✓	False ✓
There is a threat to professional behaviour.		✓
Professional ethics extend to your personal life.	✓	
Because no one else will hear, you are permitted to tell her that the take-over is not going ahead.		✓

There is a threat to confidentiality – not professional behaviour. Professional ethics does extend to your personal life. Therefore, you must not tell your friend that the takeover is not going ahead.

(e) The correct answers are:

	✓
Avoiding personal relationships with clients	✓
Complying with her firm's data protection policy	
Keeping her mind clear of prejudice and bias	✓
Behaving in a manner that does not discredit the profession	

Objectivity means avoiding prejudice, bias and maintaining impartiality. Complying with data protection policies helps maintain confidentiality. Professional behaviour is the principle where accountants must not act in a manner that discredits the profession.

Task 4

(a) **Receivables ledger**

Account name	Amount £	Debit ✓	Credit ✓
Wem Designs	1,128		✓
Bailey and Byng	354		✓

(b) **General ledger**

Account name	Amount £	Debit ✓	Credit ✓
Sales returns	1,235	✓	
VAT	247	✓	
Receivables ledger control	1,482		✓

(c) A public cloud sells services to anyone on the internet (such as Onedrive and Dropbox.) A private cloud is a proprietary network or a data centre that supplies hosted services to a limited number of people.

(d)
From: Accountingtechnician@ABC.com

To: **Khancatering@info.com**

Cc: Jacksterling@ABC.com

Subject: **The purpose of a journal, and the types of entries that can be recorded**

Date: **01/08/20XX**

Good afternoon Jessica,

My supervisor, Jack Sterling, has asked me to contact you and to answer your query regarding the purpose of a journal, and the types of entries that can be recorded.

A journal can be used to record bookkeeping transactions that may not appear in any other books of prime entry.

The entries in a journal will follow the concept of double-entry, so that journal entries are made using debits and credits to record assets, liabilities, income, expenses and capital balances.

The use of a journal can include:

1. Posting opening balances

2. Writing off irrecoverable debts

3. Recording payroll transactions

4. Correction of errors

I hope that I have answered your query on the use of journal entries.

Please do not hesitate to contact me if I can help in any other way.

Thank you,

Kind regards,

Your name

Accounting Technician

Task 5

(a) Receivables ledger control account

Details	Amount £	Debit ✓	Credit ✓
Balance owing from credit customers at 1 July	101,912	✓	
Money received from credit customers	80,435		✓
Irrecoverable debts	228		✓
Goods sold to credit customers	70,419	✓	

(b) Payables ledger control account

Details	Amount £	Debit ✓	Credit ✓
Balance owing to credit suppliers at 1 July	61,926		✓
Payment made to credit suppliers	550	✓	
Goods returned to credit suppliers	1,128	✓	

(c) The correct answer is:

	✓
Credit balance b/d on 1 September of £65,050	
Debit balance b/d on 1 September of £65,050	✓
Credit balance b/d on 1 September of £67,500	
Debit balance b/d on 1 September of £67,500	

(d) The correct answers are:

Statements	True ✓	False ✓
The payables ledger control account enables a business to identify how much is owing to credit suppliers in total.	✓	
The total of the balances in the payables ledger should reconcile with the balance of the receivables ledger control account.		✓

Task 6

(a) The correct answers are:

Statement	Correct ✓	Incorrect ✓
Consideration does not have to be sufficient or adequate.		✓
Except where the parties gain a mutual benefit, the performance of existing contractual obligations is not sufficient to support a promise of additional reward.	✓	
Executory consideration is a promise to perform an action.	✓	

Consideration must be sufficient (of some value) but need not be adequate (of equal value).

The performance of existing contractual obligations is generally not sufficient to support a promise of additional reward.

Executory consideration is a promise to do something in the future. Executed consideration is consideration provided at the time the contract is made.

(b) The correct answers are:

Statement	First reading ✓	Committee stage ✓
The bill is introduced and added to Parliament's agenda.	✓	
The bill is considered by specialists.		✓

The first reading is where the bill is introduced and added to Parliament's agenda. During the committee stage, the bill is examined by a standing committee of experts, or the whole house.

(c) The correct answers are:

Statement	True ✓	False ✓
Only reasonably foreseeable losses suffered by an injured party due to breach of contract can be recovered in damages.	✓	
Penalty clauses are a genuine pre-estimate of losses that are written into the terms of a contract.		✓

Damages will only be awarded if the losses suffered are reasonably foreseeable by the parties. If the claimant suffered an unusually high degree of loss due to the breach, the defendant will only be liable if they were aware of the claimant's special circumstances when the contract was formed.

Liquidated damages are a genuine pre-estimate of losses that are written into the terms of the contract. They are generally permitted by the courts. Penalty clauses are designed to punish the party in breach of contract and courts generally will not allow them.

Task 7

(a) Any three from the following (other relevant examples accepted):

- Breaches of confidentiality (as employees can access all information on the computer)
- Breaches of data protection legislation (due to lack of robust security of data)
- Access to information (including Luka's personal files)
- Potential theft or fraud (as employees may have access to the business bank account)
- Hacking and other cybersecurity risks (due to insecure password)

(b) The correct answer is:

	✓
Comparable	
Understandable	
Consistent	✓
Relevant and reliable	

Using the same methods and policies each time describes consistency.

(c) The correct answer is:

	✓
Until the employee leaves	
3 years	
6 years	✓
9 years	

Employee records should be kept for six years.

(d) In a manual system, the purchase is recorded in a purchases day book. This purchases day book is totalled and the total is transferred to the payables ledger control account. Every individual transaction is recorded in the individual supplier account in the payables ledger.

The same process is used to record payments to suppliers and credit notes for returns (recorded in purchases day book) which is totalled and the total recorded in the payables ledger control account. Individual transactions are then recorded in the individual supplier accounts in the payables ledger.

At the end of each period, the payables ledger is totalled and checked to the payables ledger control account total. Any errors are identified and corrected.

In a digital system, a purchase is recorded. The purchase is automatically posted to the payables ledger control account and the individual supplier account. In consequence, there are no differences between the ledger and control. Both are automatically reconciled.

Only entering the transaction once means considerable time is saved and errors reduced.

Task 8

(a) The correct answer is:

	✓
Giffen	
Inferior	✓
Substitute	

Demand for a Giffen good will increase as its price rises.

Substitutes are alternatives to each other, so that an increase in the demand for one is likely to cause a decrease in the demand for another.

(b) The correct answers are:

Statement	True ✓	False ✓
Businesses cannot avoid risk entirely.	✓	
Businesses can avoid uncertainty.		✓
Insurance is a method of mitigating risk.	✓	

Uncertainty is created where a business cannot measure or foresee an event or situation occurring.

Risk is the chance of an event occurring that causes loss or damage to a business.

Neither risk nor uncertainty can be avoided entirely. Insurance is a method of mitigating risk.

(c) The correct answer is:

	✓
The value of money will fall	
The value of money rises	✓
There is no change in the value of money	

Deflation is where there is a fall in prices generally. This means the value of money rises.

(d) The correct answers are:

	Benefit ✓	Disadvantage ✓
Access to resources	✓	
Cultural differences		✓
Market size	✓	

Trading globally means that organisations may be able to take advantage of resources that are not available in their home country or are scarce.

Globally trading businesses must manage differences in languages, time zones and culture.

The global market contains many more potential buyers than in a single country.

(e) The correct answer is:

Economy	
Fairness	
Equity	✓

Economy is the principle that the tax system should not cost an excessive amount.

The principle of fairness says that the right amount of tax should be generated at the right time. The tax system should be designed to prevent instances of double taxation and accidental non-taxation.

Equity concerns the burden of tax faced by taxpayers.

(f) The correct answers are:

Tax	Revenue ✓	Capital ✓
Income tax	✓	
Corporation tax	✓	
Inheritance tax		✓

National insurance is another revenue tax. Capital gains tax, as its name suggests, is another capital tax.

(g) The correct answers are:

Reserve requirements	✓
Taxation	
Government spending	
Interest rates	✓

The other instrument of monetary policy is exchange rates.

Tax and Government spending are instruments of fiscal policy.

BPP Practice Assessment 2

Level 2 Synoptic Assessment

Time allowed: 2 hours

Level 2 Synoptic Assessment

BPP Practice Assessment 2

Assessment information

You have **2 hours** to complete this practice assessment.

- This assessment contains **8 tasks** and you should attempt to complete **every** task.

- Each task is independent. You will not need to refer to your answers to previous tasks.

- The total number of marks for this assessment is **100**.

- Read every task carefully to make sure you understand what is required.

- Where the date is relevant, it is given in the task data.

- Both minus signs and brackets can be used to indicate negative numbers, **unless** task instructions state otherwise.

- You must use a full stop to indicate a decimal point. For example, write 100.57 **not** 100,57 or 10057.

- You may use a comma to indicate a number in the thousands, but you don't have to. For example, 10000 and 10,000 are both acceptable.

Task 1 (10 marks)

This task is about different business types and their functions.

Borderline plc was formed by two brothers over 10 years ago. They remain the only shareholders of the business.

Required

(a) Identify whether the following statements regarding how the entity concept applies for Borderline plc are true or false.

Statement	True ✓	False ✓
Only the company is liable for its debts.		
The brothers jointly own the business's assets.		
The company is required to employ directors to run the business on behalf of the brothers.		

(3 marks)

You are working in a small accountancy practice. One of the partners has asked you to provide some notes that can be added to the firm's website about partnerships.

Required

(b) Identify whether the following statements about partnerships are true or false.

Statement	True ✓	False ✓
Forming a limited liability partnership (LLP) requires submitting formal documents to the Registrar of Companies.		
Unless agreed otherwise, partners are deemed to share profits equally.		
Partners only have the right to be involved in managing the partnership if the other partners have agreed to it.		

(3 marks)

Mickey wants to buy an 'off-the-shelf' company for his next business venture.

Required

(c) Which ONE of the following statements about Mickey and his 'off-the-shelf' company is incorrect?

	✓
Mickey will still need to file registration documents with the Registrar.	
The 'off-the-shelf' company is likely to have been formed with model Articles of association.	
There will be no risk to Mickey of being liable for pre-incorporation expenses.	

(1 mark)

(d) Which function is responsible for ensuring employees have the correct mix of skills and experience?

	✓
Human resources	
Logistics	
Sales and marketing	

(1 mark)

(e) Which function identifies customer needs and makes sure the business provides them in a profitable way?

	✓
Operations	
Finance	
Sales and marketing	

(1 mark)

(f) Which function records and controls what happens to the business's money?

	✓
Finance	
Information technology	
Operations	

(1 mark)

Task 2 (13 marks)

This task is about the finance function, its information requirements and its role within the wider organisation.

The finance manager has asked you to prepare some information about the finance function to go onto the company's intranet to let all members of staff know what the function does.

Required

(a) Identify which of the following are responsible for preparing a company's statutory financial statements.

	✓
The shareholders	
The financial accountants	
The internal auditors	
The finance director	

(1 mark)

 BPP

(b) Identify which of the following parties are responsible for measuring company performance.

	✓
The management accountants	
The financial accountants	
The external auditor	
The board of directors	

(1 mark)

(c) Identify which of the following groups requires the business' monthly variance reports.

	✓
Individual department heads	
External auditors	
Payroll function	

(1 mark)

(d) Identify which of the following groups requires a business' VAT returns.

	✓
HMRC	
The shareholders	
The Government	

(1 mark)

(e) Identify which business function should receive the following information from the finance function.

Information supplied	HR ✓	Payroll ✓
Overtime worked each month		
Staff productivity levels		
Potential costs of making staff redundant		

(3 marks)

A colleague has asked for some advice on prioritising her work. Her daily tasks are as follows:

Task	Time needed for task	Description
Dealing with emails sent to finance team	1 hour	Must be completed at the start of the day
Reviewing purchase invoices	1 hour	Must be completed during the working day

 BPP

Task	Time needed for task	Description
Lunch break	1 hour	Must be taken between 12pm–1pm
Cover finance team phone line	2 × 1 hour	One hour in the morning and one hour in the afternoon

Your colleague has been asked to collect reports from department heads and deliver them to the finance director before lunch. Some of these reports will not be ready for collection until after 10.30pm. It is expected that this task will take one hour to complete.

Required

(f) **Complete the task list below by assigning each task to the correct position using the picklist.**

Task list		Time
	▼	9am–10am
	▼	10am–11am
	▼	11am–12pm
Lunch break		12pm–1pm

Picklist

- Collecting reports from department heads
- Cover finance team phone line
- Dealing with emails sent to finance team
- Reviewing purchase invoices

(3 marks)

You have recently been given several unexpected tasks to complete and are struggling to meet the deadlines set for your routine tasks.

Required

(g) **Which of the following actions should you take?**

	✓
Keep quiet and work late at night	
Book some time off for the next few days	
Inform your manager and ask for support	

(1 mark)

(h) **Identify whether the following types of information are from internal or external sources.**

Information	Internal ✓	External ✓
Credit reference agencies		
Customer account records		

(2 marks)

 BPP

Task 3 (14 marks)

This task is about corporate social responsibility (CSR), ethics and sustainability.

Required

(a) **Identify which of the following statements about sustainability are true or false.**

Statement	True ✓	False ✓
Economic sustainability concerns equal distribution of global resources.		
Social sustainability concerns working towards the eradication of human inequality, poverty and social injustice.		
Environmental sustainability concerns the need for organisations to consider how their activities impact the environment.		

(3 marks)

(b) **Identify the stakeholder from the statement using the picklist and identify whether they are internal or external stakeholders.**

Statement	Stakeholder	Internal ✓	External ✓
These stakeholders provide national infrastructure used by business.	▼		
These stakeholders expect steady, growing profits paid out of the business.	▼		

Picklist

- Directors
- Employees
- Shareholders
- The Government
- The local community
- The natural environment

(4 marks)

The AAT *Code of Professional Ethics* for accounting technicians includes five fundamental principles.

Required

(c) Which TWO of the following statements relate to the principle of objectivity?

	✓
To main professional knowledge	
To avoid bias	
To comply with relevant laws	
To act impartially	

(2 marks)

Your manager has set out a new policy that you should follow when preparing the management accounts. From now on, you are to use estimates for trade receivables and payables even though this goes against generally accepted accounting practice.

Required

(d) Identify which of the following statements concerning the situation are true or false.

Statement	True ✓	False ✓
There is a threat to your integrity.		
You cannot be in breach of professional ethics if you are following a company policy.		
Your manager is acting in breach of the fundamental ethical principles.		

(3 marks)

Jerome is a student member of AAT and has been asked by his manager to send copies of a client's draft accounts to their bank because the bank is concerned that the client may not be able to repay a loan.

Required

(e) Identify TWO correct statements regarding the situation.

	✓
Potential breach of contract, such as defaulting on a loan, is a circumstance where Jerome has a professional right to disclose confidential information.	
Jerome can disclose confidential information, such as the draft accounts, where disclosure is required by law and is authorised by the client.	
Jerome can disclose the draft accounts because the bank will have its own duty to maintain confidentiality on behalf of the client.	
Jerome can disclose confidential information if there is a professional duty to do so which is in the public interest and not prohibited by law.	

(2 marks)

 BPP

Task 4 (22 marks)

This task is about processing bookkeeping transactions and communicating information.

You are employed by Judson Ltd. Below is a summary of Judson Ltd's account in a customer's purchase ledger (Gold Ltd). Judson Ltd has agreed to allow Gold Ltd to make payments by the last day of the second month following the month of invoice. Invoices issued in January will be due for payment by 31 March, for example.

Date 20XX	Details	Amount £
1 April	Invoice J338	1,145
3 April	Invoice J345	1,330
7 May	Invoice J401	2,887
7 May	Credit note C025	1,330
26 May	Credit note C033	236
26 May	Invoice J478	7,216
26 June	Invoice J501	442
30 June	Credit note C040	152

Required

(a) Complete the table below by:

- **Entering the total of transactions with Judson Ltd in each of the months April, May and June.**

- **Selecting the dates by which payments should be made by circling the relevant dates.**

Month	Amount £	Payments to be made by
Transactions in April		▼
Transactions in May		▼
Transactions in June		▼

Picklist

- 30 April
- 30 June
- 31 August
- 31 July
- 31 May

(6 marks)

Your manager, Josie Marina, has sent you the memo below which you have received today, 1 November 20XX.

 BPP

Memo

As you are aware, we have a special payment arrangement with Gold Ltd, an important customer. We have agreed to allow Gold Ltd to make payments by the last day of the second month following the month of invoice. The payment terms for other customers are 30 days.

Unfortunately, Gold Ltd has been late with payment on the last two scheduled payment dates.

Please prepare a letter, addressed to Gold Ltd, explaining when payments should be made, and stating that we may have to reconsider our payment arrangement if future payments are not made by their due date.

Our contact at Gold Ltd is Mr Carat, and I would be grateful if you would sign the letter on behalf of our company.

Many thanks,

Josie

Required

(b)   Prepare a suitable business letter to Gold Ltd, making sure your letter is dated the same date as Josie's memo.

Judson Ltd

28 Anderson Street, Ainsley, AN21 8EN

Telephone: 01872 890120

Email: judson@sales.com

Mr Carat

Gold Ltd

14 High Street

Darton, DF11 4GX

(10 marks)

On a separate matter, Josie Marina has contacted you about an interesting project she is involved in. The company is looking into introducing cloud accounting at the company and she has asked you for your thoughts on it.

 BPP

Required

(c) State four benefits of cloud accounting. (4 marks)

Judson Ltd has received a cheque for £1,512 from a credit customer, B Cohen, in full settlement of the account. There was no document included with the cheque to show what transactions were included in the payment.

Required

(d) Identify the document the customer should have included with the cheque.

	✓
Delivery note	
Petty cash voucher	
Purchase order	
Remittance advice note	

(2 marks)

Task 5 (10 marks)

This task is about control accounts, reconciliations and using journals to correct accounts.

You work in the accounts team at Haven Ltd. You have been notified that a credit customer, Jae Pih, has ceased trading, owing Haven Ltd £2,320 plus VAT.

Required

(a) Record the journal entries needed in the general ledger to write off the net amount and the VAT.

Account name	Amount £	Debit ✓	Credit ✓
▼			
▼			
▼			

Picklist

- Haven
- Irrecoverable debts
- Jae Pih
- Payables ledger control
- Purchases
- Receivables ledger control
- Sales
- VAT

(6 marks)

It is important to understand the types of error that are disclosed by the trial balance and those that are not.

Required

(b) Show which of the errors below are, or are not, disclosed by the trial balance.

Errors	Error disclosed by the trial balance ✓	Error NOT disclosed by the trial balance ✓
Recording a bank payment for office expenses on the debit side of the office furniture account.		
Recording a payment for motor expenses in the bank account, the motor expenses account and the miscellaneous expenses account (Ignore VAT.)		
Recording a payment by cheque to a credit supplier in the bank account and payables ledger control account only.		

(3 marks)

One of the errors in (b) above can be classified as an error of principle.

Required

(c) Show which error is an error of principle.

	✓
Recording a bank payment for office expenses on the debit side of the office furniture account	
Recording a payment for motor expenses in the bank account, the motor expenses account and the miscellaneous expenses account (Ignore VAT)	
Recording a payment by cheque to a credit supplier in the bank account and payables ledger control account only	

(1 mark)

Task 6 (7 marks)

This task is about the principles of contract law.

Required

(a) Match the following statements to the correct track in the civil law system.

Statement	Fast track ✓	Multi-track ✓
Hears cases that are expected to last under a day		
Hears cases at the High Court		

(2 marks)

Required

(b) Identify whether the following statements regarding consideration are correct or incorrect.

Statement	Correct ✓	Incorrect ✓
Consideration must be provided at the time the contract is made or afterwards.		
Executed consideration is an act given in return for a promise.		

(2 marks)

Wiston Ltd has contracted with Prof Ltd to buy scientific equipment with delivery due in August. Payment was due a week after delivery. In July, Prof Ltd had almost completed production of the equipment when Wiston Ltd sent notification that it no longer required the equipment and would not be paying for it.

Required

(c) Which of the following statements are true or false?

Statement	True ✓	False ✓
Wiston Ltd has committed repudiatory breach of contract.		
Prof Ltd must continue to perform its obligations and deliver the equipment in August.		
Wiston Ltd will not have to pay damages because it notified Prof Ltd that it does not need the goods before the delivery date.		

(3 marks)

Task 7 (10 marks)

This task is about bookkeeping systems, receipts and payments, as well as the importance of information and data security.

Nila runs a business with her brother, Zak, and ten employees. She is keen to make sure all business data is held safely and securely and is developing some policies for the business covering data security.

Required

(a) State THREE policies that Nila could adopt. (3 marks)

Zak helps Nila by preparing reports about the performance of the business to make better business decisions. Zak only includes information that Nila needs for her decision in his reports.

Required

(b) Which characteristic of useful information does Zak apply?

	✓
Comparable	
Understandable	
Consistent	
Relevant and reliable	

(1 mark)

(c) How long should Nila keep banking records for?

	✓
Until she changes banks	
3 years	
6 years	
9 years	

(1 mark)

Nila is thinking of introducing a cloud-based accounting system that records business transactions digitally. Previously, she operated a manual system for recording business transactions.

Required

(d) Using the example of a sale to a customer, explain how the two systems for recording transactions differ.

Your answer should refer to the books of prime entry, the receivables ledger and the receivables ledger control account. (5 marks)

Task 8 (14 marks)

This task is about the external business environment.

Heath Tech Ltd is a successful business in its home country and is thinking of expanding overseas. The business understands that there is risk and uncertainty involved in trading globally and that the PESTEL model is one method of identifying sources of risk and uncertainty.

Required

(a) Which of the following factors does the 'T' in PESTEL relate to?

	✓
Taxation	
Technology	
Trade	

(1 mark)

(b) Identify whether the following statements regarding uncertainty and risk are true or false.

Statement	True ✓	False ✓
Business policies and procedures can eliminate business risk.		
Disaster planning is a method of mitigating risk.		
Uncertainty can occur when the impact of a potential event cannot be measured.		

(3 marks)

(c) Which of the following statements is correct regarding inflation?

	✓
The value of money will fall.	
The value of money rises.	
There is no change in the value of money.	

(1 mark)

(d) Identify whether the following factors affect demand or supply of a product.

Factor	Affects demand ✓	Affects supply ✓
Income levels		
Changes in technology		
Fashion and expectations		

(3 marks)

(e) Which of the following is a principle of an effective tax system?

	✓
Accuracy	
Convenience	
Timeliness	

(1 mark)

(f) Identify whether the following taxes are direct or indirect taxes.

Tax	Direct ✓	Indirect ✓
Income tax		
Corporation tax		
VAT		

(3 marks)

(g) **Identify TWO instruments of fiscal policy.**

	✓
Government spending	
Exchange rates	
Interest rates	
Taxation	

(2 marks)

BPP Practice Assessment 2

Level 2 Synoptic Assessment

Answers

Task 1

(a) The correct answers are:

Statement	True ✓	False ✓
Only the company is liable for its debts.	✓	
The brothers jointly own the business's assets.		✓
The company is required to employ directors to run the business on behalf of the brothers.		✓

As a separate legal entity, the company owns its assets and is the only party liable for its debts.

The brothers could decide to employ directors, but there is nothing stopping them being directors and shareholders.

(b) The correct answers are:

Statement	True ✓	False ✓
Forming a limited liability partnership (LLP) requires submitting formal documents to the Registrar of Companies.	✓	
Unless agreed otherwise, partners are deemed to share profits equally.	✓	
Partners only have the right to be involved in managing the partnership if the other partners have agreed to it.		✓

Forming an LLP requires documents to be submitted to the Registrar of Companies. Unless agreed otherwise, partners have an equal stake in the profits of the firm and are to be involved in managing the partnership.

(c) The correct answer is:

	✓
Mickey will still need to file registration documents with the Registrar.	✓
The 'off-the-shelf' company is likely to have been formed with model Articles of association.	
There will be no risk to Mickey of being liable for pre-incorporation expenses.	

As 'off-the-shelf' companies have already been formed, no registration documents need to be filed and there is no risk of liability for pre-incorporation expenses. Such companies are usually formed with model Articles of association.

(d) The correct answer is:

	✓
Human resources	✓
Logistics	
Sales and marketing	

ANSWERS

(e) The correct answer is:

	✓
Operations	
Finance	
Sales and marketing	✓

(f) The correct answer is:

	✓
Finance	✓
Information technology	
Operations	

The statements are the roles that each of the identified business functions have.

Task 2

(a) The correct answer is:

	✓
The shareholders	
The financial accountants	✓
The internal auditors	
The finance director	

(b) The correct answer is:

	✓
The management accountants	✓
The financial accountants	
The external auditor	
The board of directors	

The financial accountants are responsible for preparing the financial statements which will then be audited by the external auditors. Management accounting information prepared by the management accountants helps measure company performance.

(c) The correct answer is:

	✓
Individual department heads	✓
External auditors	
Payroll function	

(d) The correct answer is:

	✓
HMRC	✓
The shareholders	
The Government	

Individual department heads need monthly variance reports to check that their function is operating as expected.

VAT returns are submitted to HMRC.

(e) The correct answers are:

Information supplied	HR ✓	Payroll ✓
Overtime worked each month		✓
Staff productivity levels	✓	
Potential costs of making staff redundant	✓	

Overtime work needs to be given to payroll to ensure staff are paid the correct amount each month.

Productivity levels and costs of redundancies are required by HR to make staffing decisions.

(f)

Task list	Time
Dealing with emails sent to finance team	9am–10am
Cover finance team phone line	10am–11am
Collecting reports from department heads	11am–12pm
Lunch break	12pm–1pm

Dealing with emails sent to the finance team must be done at the start of the day. The next choice is whether to cover the finance team's phone line or start collecting reports. However, the reports may not be ready until after 10.30am so the priority is to cover the phone line. The reports can be collected from 11am when they should all be ready and can be delivered to the finance director before lunch. Reviewing the purchase invoices can be done after lunch.

(g) The correct answer is:

	✓
Keep quiet and work late at night	
Book some time off for the next few days	
Inform your manager and ask for support	✓

You should always inform your manager and ask for support if you are struggling with deadlines. They may be able to lighten up your workload or provide extra time or resources to get tasks done.

BPP

(h) The correct answers are:

Information	Internal ✓	External ✓
Credit reference agencies		✓
Customer account records	✓	

Credit reference agencies are outside of an organisation. Customer account records are found in an organisation's own computer system

Task 3

(a) The correct answers are:

Statement	True ✓	False ✓
Economic sustainability concerns equal distribution of global resources.		✓
Social sustainability concerns working towards the eradication of human inequality, poverty and social injustice.	✓	
Environmental sustainability concerns the need for organisations to consider how their activities impact the environment.	✓	

Economic sustainability ensures fair (not necessarily equal) distribution and efficient allocation of global resources.

Social sustainability involves the responsibility to work towards eradication of human inequality, poverty and social injustice.

Environmental sustainability describes the need for organisations to consider how their activities impact the environment and to take steps to minimise that impact and to conserve energy.

(b)

Statement	Stakeholder	Internal ✓	External ✓
These stakeholders provide national infrastructure used by business.	The Government		✓
These stakeholders expect steady, growing profits paid out of the business.	Shareholders	✓	

The Government provides the national infrastructure used by business and is an external stakeholder.

Shareholders expect a return on the money they have invested in the business in the form of steady, growing profits and/or capital growth of the shares.

(c) The correct answers are:

	✓
To main professional knowledge	
To avoid bias	✓
To comply with relevant laws	
To act impartially	✓

Objectivity is the principle that all professional and business judgements should be made fairly:

- On the basis of an independent and intellectually honest appraisal of information

- Free from all forms of prejudice and bias

- Free from factors which might affect impartiality

Maintaining professional knowledge is required to meet the principle of professional competence and due care.

Complying with laws and regulations is required to comply with professional behaviour.

(d) The correct answers are:

Statement	True ✓	False ✓
There is a threat to your integrity.	✓	
You cannot be in breach of professional ethics if you are following a company policy.		✓
Your manager is acting in breach of the fundamental ethical principles.	✓	

Integrity is the important principle of honesty and requires accountants to be straightforward in all professional and business relationships. It also means not being party to the supply of false or misleading information. The continued use of estimates risks inaccurate trade receivables and payables and, therefore, misleading accounts.

You must follow the profession's ethical principles even if it goes against a company policy.

Your manager is acting in breach of professional behaviour by requiring you to breach the principle of integrity.

(e) The correct answers are:

	✓
Potential breach of contract, such as defaulting on a loan, is a circumstance where Jerome has a professional right to disclose confidential information.	
Jerome can disclose confidential information, such as the draft accounts, where disclosure is required by law and is authorised by the client.	✓
Jerome can disclose the draft accounts because the bank will have its own duty to maintain confidentiality on behalf of the client.	
Jerome can disclose confidential information if there is a professional duty to do so which is in the public interest and not prohibited by law.	✓

There are only two circumstances where an accountant can breach the principle of confidentiality:

(1) Where disclosure is required by law, and is authorised by the client or the employer

(2) Where there is a professional right or duty to disclose which is in the public interest and is not prohibited by law

Task 4

(a)

Month	Amount £	Payments to be made by
Transactions in April	2,475	30 June
Transactions in May	8,537	31 July
Transactions in June	290	31 August

(b)

Judson Ltd

28 Anderson Street, Ainsley, AN21 8EN

Telephone: 01872 890120

Email: judson@sales.com

Mr Carat
Gold Ltd
14 High Street
Darton, DF11 4GX

1 November 20XX

Dear Mr Carat,

Late payments

Our records show that your business has been late with its last two scheduled payments to us.

I must remind you that, under the terms of our agreement, payment is expected on the last day of the second month following the month when a sale is invoiced. So, for example, invoices issued by us in November will be due for payment by 31 January.

If you do not pay in accordance with these agreed terms, then we will have to request that all future invoices are settled on our usual terms of business, which is 30 days from the invoice date.

Please let me know if you have any questions regarding our payment terms, or if I can help in any way.

Your sincerely,

(Your name)

Accounting Technician

(c) The main benefits of a cloud accounting system over a traditional system installed on individual machines include (any four from):

- System data and the software itself are automatically refreshed and kept up-to-date.

- Information in the system is available to multiple users simultaneously and globally, as long as the users have internet access and a login.

- Duplication and other system errors and inconsistencies are eliminated because only one set of data is kept and is synchronised to all users.
- Data is stored in one offsite location and users simply access the information when required. There is no need to transmit the data between users over the internet or by USB stick, increasing data security.
- Multiple users mean key people can access financial and customer details should they need to.
- It reduces the cost and complexity of keeping backups of the data because this is performed by the cloud service provider.
- It reduces the cost and time involved in upgrading the software.
- It improves support and customer service because the service provider can access the user's information to help resolve issues.

(d) The correct answer is:

	✓
Delivery note	
Petty cash voucher	
Purchase order	
Remittance advice note	✓

Task 5

(a)

Account name	Amount £	Debit ✓	Credit ✓
Irrecoverable debts	2,320	✓	
VAT	464	✓	
Receivables ledger control	2,784		✓

(b) The correct answers are:

Errors	Error disclosed by the trial balance ✓	Error NOT disclosed by the trial balance ✓
Recording a bank payment for office expenses on the debit side of the office furniture account.		✓
Recording a payment for motor expenses in the bank account, the motor expenses account and the miscellaneous expenses account (Ignore VAT.)	✓	
Recording a payment by cheque to a credit supplier in the bank account and payables ledger control account only.		✓

 BPP

ANSWERS

(c) The correct answer is:

	✓
Recording a bank payment for office expenses on the debit side of the office furniture account	✓
Recording a payment for motor expenses in the bank account, the motor expenses account and the miscellaneous expenses account (Ignore VAT)	
Recording a payment by cheque to a credit supplier in the bank account and payables ledger control account only	

Task 6

(a) The correct answers are:

Statement	Fast track ✓	Multi-track ✓
Hears cases that are expected to last under a day	✓	
Hears cases at the High Court		✓

The fast track deals with cases with a value between £10,000 and £25,000 that will last for a day or less. Cases are heard at the Country Court.

Multi-track cases have a value of over £25,000 or are complex, and are heard at the High Court.

(b) The correct answers are:

Statement	Correct ✓	Incorrect ✓
Consideration must be provided at the time the contract is made or afterwards.	✓	
Executed consideration is an act given in return for a promise.		✓

Consideration provided before the contract was made is past consideration and is generally not valid. Executed consideration is consideration provided at the time the contract is made and is an act done in return for a promise. Executory consideration is a promise to do something in the future.

(c) The correct answers are:

Statement	True ✓	False ✓
Wiston Ltd has committed repudiatory breach of contract.		✓
Prof Ltd must continue to perform its obligations and deliver the equipment in August.		✓
Wiston Ltd will not have to pay damages because it notified Prof Ltd that it does not need the goods before the delivery date.		✓

 BPP

Wiston Ltd has committed anticipatory breach of contract. This occurs when a party declares that they will break the terms of the contract before the time for performance has arrived.

Due to Wiston Ltd's breach of contract, Prof Ltd may treat the contract as discharged and is not required to perform its obligations under it. The breach of contract allows Prof Ltd to recover damages for any losses it has incurred.

Task 7

(a) Any three from the following:

- The non-removal of data and equipment from the premises
- The frequent backing-up of computerised data, and the storage of backups separately from the original data, so that there are safe copies in case of systems failure, data corruption or fire
- The use of anti-virus software, firewalls and other protective tools on all computers, to prevent malicious corruption and theft of data
- The use of passwords to restrict access to computer systems or files (often with additional policies regarding the complexity and regular change of passwords) to prevent unauthorised users from obtaining, amending or deleting them
- The use of authorisations to control access to security-coded paper-based files
- The non-divulging of passwords, security codes and other data security measures to other parties

(b) The correct answer is:

	✓
Comparable	
Understandable	
Consistent	
Relevant and reliable	✓

Only providing information needed to make a decision describes relevant and reliable.

(c) The correct answer is:

	✓
Until she changes banks	
3 years	
6 years	✓
9 years	

Banking records should be kept for six years.

(d) In a manual system, the sale is recorded in a sales day book. This sales day book is totalled and the total is transferred to the receivables ledger control account. Every individual transaction is recorded in the individual customer account in the receivables ledger.

The same process is used to record payments from customers and credit notes issued for returns (recorded in sales day book) which is totalled and the total recorded in the receivables ledger control account). Individual transactions are then recorded in the individual customer accounts in the receivables ledger.

At the end of each period, the receivables ledger is totalled and checked to the receivables ledger control account total. Any errors are identified and corrected.

In a digital system, a sale is recorded. The sale is automatically posted to the receivables ledger control account and the individual customer account. Consequently, there are no differences between the ledger and control. Both are automatically reconciled.

Only entering the transaction once means considerable time is saved and errors reduced.

Task 8

(a) The correct answer is:

	✓
Taxation	
Technology	✓
Trade	

The other PESTEL factors are Political, Economic, Social, Environmental and Legal.

(b) The correct answers are:

Statement	True ✓	False ✓
Business policies and procedures can eliminate business risk.		✓
Disaster planning is a method of mitigating risk.	✓	
Uncertainty can occur when the impact of a potential event cannot be measured.	✓	

Nothing can eliminate business risk entirely.

Along with insurance, disaster planning is a method of mitigating business risk.

Uncertainty also occurs because a business cannot foresee an event or situation occurring.

(c) The correct answer is:

	✓
The value of money will fall.	✓
The value of money rises.	
There is no change in the value of money.	

Inflation is where there is a rise in prices generally. This means the value of money falls.

(d) The correct answers are:

Factor	Affects demand ✓	Affects supply ✓
Income levels	✓	
Changes in technology		✓

Factor	Affects demand ✓	Affects supply ✓
Fashion and expectations	✓	

Consumer income will impact on how much of a good will be demanded. Demand can increase or even fall depending on the type of good.

Technology can cause an increase in supply due to a production process becoming more efficient or effective.

A change in fashion or tastes will alter the demand for a product. For example, if it becomes fashionable for households in the UK to drink wine with their meals, expenditure on wine will increase.

(e) The correct answer is:

	✓
Accuracy	
Convenience	✓
Timeliness	

The principle of convenience says that the tax system should make it easy for taxpayers to comply with the rules and pay the right amount of tax due.

(f) The correct answers are:

Tax	Direct ✓	Indirect ✓
Income tax	✓	
Corporation tax	✓	
VAT		✓

In the UK, most taxes are direct, but VAT is an exception.

(g) The correct answers are:

	✓
Government spending	✓
Exchange rates	
Interest rates	
Taxation	✓

Fiscal policy involves taxation and Government spending. Interest and exchange rates plus reserve requirements are instruments of monetary policy.

BPP Practice Assessment 3

Level 2 Synoptic Assessment

Time allowed: 2 hours

Level 2 Synoptic Assessment

BPP Practice Assessment 3

Assessment information

You have **2 hours** to complete this practice assessment.

- This assessment contains **8 tasks** and you should attempt to complete **every** task.

- Each task is independent. You will not need to refer to your answers to previous tasks.

- The total number of marks for this assessment is **100**.

- Read every task carefully to make sure you understand what is required.

- Where the date is relevant, it is given in the task data.

- Both minus signs and brackets can be used to indicate negative numbers, **unless** task instructions state otherwise.

- You must use a full stop to indicate a decimal point. For example, write 100.57 **not** 100,57 or 10057.

- You may use a comma to indicate a number in the thousands, but you don't have to. For example, 10000 and 10,000 are both acceptable.

Task 1 (10 marks)

This task is about different business types and their functions.

Required

(a) Identify whether the following statements regarding entities and the entity concept are true or false.

Statement	True ✓	False ✓
An entity is a function of a business.		
Entities have no basis in law.		
The financial accounts of an entity should only reflect the business activities and its financial performance, not that of its owners.		

(3 marks)

A friend is thinking of starting up in business as a sole trader and has some questions.

Required

(b) Identify whether the followings statements about sole traders are true or false.

Statement	True ✓	False ✓
A sole trader has complete control over the business.		
Sole traders are not permitted to employ staff.		
Sole traders do not have to share their profits with anyone.		

(3 marks)

(c) Which of the following is a tax that all limited liability partnerships must account for and pay?

	✓
Corporation tax	
VAT	
Income tax	

(1 mark)

(d) Which function of a business performs sales support?

	✓
Marketing	
Operations	
Human resources	

(1 mark)

(e) Which function of a business disciplines employees?

	✓
Human resources	
Finance	
Logistics	

(1 mark)

(f) Which function of a business adds value to products and services?

	✓
Operations	
Information technology	
Finance	

(1 mark)

Task 2 (13 marks)

This task is about the finance function, its information requirements and its role within the wider organisation.

You have recently received a promotion to assistant accountant to reflect the fact that you have nearly completed your AAT training. The finance manager has asked you to prepare some information about the finance function to help new starters in the team.

Required

(a) Identify which of the following parties are responsible for signing an audit report.

	✓
The finance director	
The shareholders	
The external auditors	
The internal auditors	

(1 mark)

(b) Identify which of the following parties are responsible for keeping the company's accounting records.

	✓
The financial accountants	
The management accountants	
The Registrar of Companies	
The payroll function	

(1 mark)

(c) Identify TWO principles of effective communication which should be followed by the finance function.

	✓
Honest	
Accurate	
Available	
Timely	
Efficient	
Planned	

(2 marks)

(d) Identify which of the following activities of the finance function are relevant to solvency and legal compliance of the organisation.

Activity	Solvency ✓	Legal compliance ✓
Monitoring the organisation's cash flow		
Forecasting the organisation's working capital requirements		
Correctly calculating tax liabilities		

(3 marks)

It is Monday morning and you have been given some unexpected tasks to complete as follows:

Task	Time needed for task	Other information
Prepare a report needed by the finance director	1 hour	Needed by lunchtime
Prepare costing calculations needed by the operations director	1 hour	Needed by tomorrow morning
Shredding old purchase invoices	1 hour	To be done by the end of the week

Your lunch break is between 12pm and 1pm. Your routine tasks (which will take an hour in total) must be completed within the working day and involve processing invoices and responding to emails.

Required

(e) Complete the task list below by selecting the appropriate tasks from the picklist provided.

Task list	Order of task completion
▼	First task
▼	Second task
▼	Third task

Picklist

- Prepare a report needed by the finance director
- Prepare costing calculations needed by the operations director
- Routine tasks
- Shredding old purchase invoices

(3 marks)

Your manager has asked you to prepare a draft set of management accounts for a meeting in two days' time. Due to staff illness and holidays, you are the only person with the knowledge and experience to do this. However, it will mean that you do not have time to complete the routine tasks that you share with other members of your team.

Required

(f) **Which of the following actions should you take?**

	✓
Refuse to take on the extra work.	
Do the extra work and ignore your routine tasks.	
Speak to your manager about delegating your routine tasks to others while you do the extra work.	

(1 mark)

(g) **Identify whether the following statements about information are true or false.**

Statement	True ✓	False ✓
Accurate information can become inaccurate over time.		
Information is valid if it is appropriate to the use it is being put to.		

(2 marks)

Task 3 (14 marks)

This task is about corporate social responsibility (CSR), ethics and sustainability.

Required

(a) **Identify which of the following statements about corporate social responsibility (CSR) are true or false.**

Statement	True ✓	False ✓
The objective of CSR policies is to improve the public's perception of the business.		
Individuals working within an organisation have a duty to act in accordance with CSR principles.		
Triple bottom line reporting applies only to business activities that affect the environment.		

(3 marks)

 BPP

(b) **Identify the stakeholder from the statement and identify whether they are internal or external stakeholders.**

Statement	Stakeholder	Internal ✓	External ✓
These stakeholders expect fair and growing remuneration.	▼		
These stakeholders expect continuity of custom.	▼		

Picklist

- Customers
- Employees
- Lenders
- Local community
- Shareholders
- Suppliers

(4 marks)

The AAT *Code of Professional Ethics* for accounting technicians includes five fundamental principles.

Required

(c) **Which TWO of the following statements relate to the principle of professional behaviour?**

	✓
To comply with relevant laws	
To act honestly	
To avoid conduct that discredits the profession	
To avoid conflicts of interest	

(2 marks)

Jenny is a student member of the AAT who is studying for her exams whilst working in an accountancy and tax practice. Her father has asked her to calculate inheritance tax due on an estate that he has recently inherited. Jenny has studied inheritance tax but has not yet taken a tax exam.

Required

(d) **Identify which of the following statements concerning the situation are true or false.**

Statement	True ✓	False ✓
If Jenny waits until she has passed a tax exam, she will be deemed competent to perform the calculation.		
As this is a private, family matter, professional ethics do not apply.		
There is a familiarity threat to Jenny.		

(3 marks)

 BPP

(e) Identify TWO actions that Jenny could take from the following list.

	✓
Tell her father she is not professionally competent to perform the calculation.	
Refer her father to a tax specialist at work.	
Refuse to do the calculation — there is no need to give a reason.	
Perform the calculation but check her calculation afterwards.	

(2 marks)

Task 4 (22 marks)

This task is about processing bookkeeping transactions and communicating information.

You are an accounts clerk working for Donut Ltd and work on both receivables and payables accounts. Today, purchase invoices and purchase credit notes have been received and partially entered in the day books, as shown below.

Required

(a) Complete the entries in the purchases day book and the purchases returns day book by:

- Selecting the correct supplier account codes from the coding list below
- Inserting the appropriate figures to complete the entries

Coding list

Supplier name	Supplier account code
Cox and Co	COX001
GBL Ltd	GBL001
R King	KIN001
JAB Ltd	JAB001
Jackson plc	JAC002
Johnson Ltd	JOH003
PDL Designs	PDL001
K Ponti	PON002
Proctor Ltd	PRO003

Purchases day book

Date	Details	Supplier account code	Invoice number	Total	VAT	Net	Product A100	Product B100
20XX				£	£	£	£	£
30 Jun	GBL Ltd	▼	G1161	348		290		290
30 Jun	Jackson plc	▼	4041		125		625	
30 Jun	R King	▼	J1126	612			275	235

 BPP

Purchases returns day book

Date 20XX	Details	Supplier account code	Credit note number	Total £	VAT £	Net £	Product A100 £	Product B100 £
30 Jun	PDL Designs	▼	CN110				560	200
30 Jun	K Ponti	▼	398C		95		225	250

Picklist

- COX001
- GBL001
- JAB001
- JAC002
- JOH003
- KIN001
- PDL001
- PON002
- PRO003

(5 marks)

Jason is a new member of staff and, during his induction, he asked you the purpose of having a coding system for customers and suppliers.

It is the morning of 1 October and you are drafting an email in response to Jason.

Required

(b) Complete the email below to answer Jason's query regarding coding systems for customers and suppliers.

From:
To: Jason@XYZ.com
Cc:
Subject: Purpose of coding systems
Date: 01/10/20XX

 BPP

(10 marks)

Your manager is investigating the potential use of cloud accounting at Donut Ltd.

Required

(c) State four potential problems of cloud accounting. (4 marks)

You have been given details of a number of purchases made for cash inclusive of VAT at 20%.

Required

(d) Calculate the amount of VAT on each purchase and the net amount of the purchase.

Gross total	VAT	Net total
£	£	£
277.24		
163.42		
49.74		

(3 marks)

Task 5 (10 marks)

This task is about control accounts, reconciliations and using journals to correct accounts.

You work for Goldbloom Ltd in the financial accounts team. You have begun working on the latest set of accounts but found when the trial balance was extracted it did not balance. The debit column of the trial balance totalled £395,222 and the credit column totalled £395,141.

Required

(a) Record the journal entry needed in the suspense account to balance the trial balance and, in the general ledger, to remove the suspense account balance arising from the error in the cash book.

Account name	Amount £	Debit ✓	Credit ✓
Suspense			

Account name	Amount £	Debit ✓	Credit ✓
▼			

Picklist

- Balance b/f
- Balance c/d
- Bank
- Cahs purchases
- Suspense
- Total
- Trade payables

(4 marks)

The error in the trial balance has now been identified as arising from an incorrectly totalled VAT column in the cash book, as shown below.

Cash book

Date 20XX	Details	Bank £	Date 20XX	Details	Bank £	VAT £	Trade payables £	Cash purchases £
30 June	Balance b/f	14,197	30 Jun	James Jones	654	109		545
30 June	Baker and Co	1,445	30 Jun	BDL Ltd	6,197		6,197	
			30 Jun	Connor Smith	474	79		395
			30 Jun	Balance c/d	8,317			
	Total	15,642		Totals	15,642	269	6,197	940

Required

(b) Record the journal entry needed in the general ledger to remove the incorrect entry from the cash book.

Account name	Amount £	Debit ✓	Credit ✓
VAT			

(2 marks)

(c) Record the journal entry needed in the general ledger to record the correct entry that should have been made in the cash book.

 BPP

Account name	Amount £	Debit ✓	Credit ✓
VAT			

(2 marks)

(d) Identify one use for journal entries.

	✓
To detect fraud	
To record goods bought on credit	
To record goods sold on credit	
To record non-regular transactions	

(2 marks)

Task 6 (7 marks)

This task is about the principles of contract law.

Required

(a) Identify whether the following statements apply to public or private law.

Statement	Public law ✓	Private law ✓
A framework of rules provided by Parliament to provide individuals with a system to settle disputes.		
Concerns how government and local councils operate but also covers criminal law.		

(2 marks)

(b) Identify which of the following statements are valid offers.

Statement	Valid offer ✓	Not a valid offer ✓
Goods displayed in a shop window		
Public advertisements		

(2 marks)

(c) Identify whether the following statements concerning remedies for breach of contract are correct or incorrect.

Statement	Correct ✓	Incorrect ✓
Equitable remedies are awarded if requested by the claimant.		
Damages are an equitable remedy.		
Damages are generally only payable for economic losses.		

(3 marks)

 BPP

Task 7 (10 marks)

This task is about bookkeeping systems, receipts and payments, as well as the importance of information and data security.

Hatchem Ltd is a company that makes and sells small toys for children. The company has a strong online presence and has worked hard to build trust with its customers and suppliers over time.

Alex is the finance director of Hatchem Ltd. Following a review by an internet expert, he has been warned that the business could be the victim of a cyber-attack in the near future.

Required

(a) State THREE risks to the business that might be caused by a cyberattack. (3 marks)

Josh has recently been employed by Hatchem Ltd as a management accountant. Last week, he reviewed the past twelve months of management accounts to understand how the business has been performing. However, he found that many of the policies and calculations used in calculating the figures in accounts change each month to make sure the results look good.

Required

(b) Which characteristic of useful information is missing from Hatchem Ltd's management accounts?

	✓
Relevant and reliable	
Understandable	
Comparable	
Timely	

(1 mark)

(c) Which of the following information produced by the finance team can be used by management to learn from past mistakes and improve performance in the future?

	✓
Corporate tax payable	
Variance reports	
Details of cash balances	
Customer account statements	

(1 mark)

Luka is thinking of introducing a cloud-based accounting system that records business transactions digitally. Previously, he operated a manual system for recording business transactions.

Required

(d) Describe how automation and artificial intelligence can benefit accountants and auditors.

(5 marks)

Task 8 (14 marks)

This task is about the external business environment.

Lincolnwood Ltd is currently only trading within its home country but is concerned about risk and uncertainty and the global market.

Required

(a) Which of the following statements is correct?

	✓
The company can protect itself from global risk and uncertainty by only trading in its home country.	
The company cannot avoid all risk and uncertainty from the global market.	
The company can buy insurance to protect itself from global risks generally.	

(1 mark)

(b) Identify whether the following statements regarding the equilibrium price are true or false.

Statement	True ✓	False ✓
The equilibrium price is the price of a good where the volume demanded by customers and the volume supplied by businesses are the same.		
Once established, the equilibrium price for a market is fixed.		
The equilibrium price is the average price charged for a good in the market.		

(3 marks)

(c) Which of the following statements is correct regarding the profit motive?

	✓
The profit motive describes the purpose of organisations to make their owners wealthier.	
All business organisations are motivated by profit.	
Making short-term losses is inconsistent with the profit motive.	

(1 mark)

(d) Identify whether the following statements relate to progressive, regressive or proportional rates of tax.

	Progressive ✓	Regressive ✓	Proportional ✓
The tax rate decreases as the amount to be taxed increases.			
The tax rate increases as the amount to be taxed increases.			
The tax rate is always the same regardless of the level of income.			

(3 marks)

(e) Which of the following principles of an effective tax system states that taxes should be clear and easy to understand and calculate?

	✓
Transparency	
Certainty	
Fairness	

(1 mark)

(f) Identify whether the following statements relate to micro or macro-economics.

Statement	Micro-economics ✓	Macro-economics ✓
Relates to a specific industry		
Concerned with issues such as employment levels and inflation		
Helps a business decide how much of a product to make		

(3 marks)

Governments can use fiscal policy to change the level of aggregate demand in the economy.

Required

(g) Which TWO fiscal policies should reduce the level of aggregate demand in an economy?

	✓
Reduce tax but do not reduce government spending	
Increase taxation	
Increase government spending but do not alter taxation	
Reduce government spending	

(2 marks)

BPP Practice Assessment 3

Level 2 Synoptic Assessment

Answers

Task 1

(a) The correct answers are:

Statement	True ✓	False ✓
An entity is a function of a business.		✓
Entities have no basis in law.		✓
The financial accounts of an entity should only reflect the business activities and its financial performance, not that of its owners.	✓	

The entity concept applies to a whole business, not business functions. It is a legal concept that allows, for example, a business to own its assets and be liable for its debts. An entity's financial accounts should only reflect its business activities and its financial performance, not the finances of its owners.

(b) The correct answers are:

Statement	True ✓	False ✓
A sole trader has complete control over the business.	✓	
Sole traders are not permitted to employ staff.		✓
Sole traders do not have to share their profits with anyone.	✓	

Sole traders are free to run the business themselves as they see fit; all profits accrue to them. They may employ staff if they wish.

(c) The correct answer is:

	✓
Corporation tax	
VAT	
Income tax	✓

LLPs are liable to pay income tax and national insurance on behalf of their employees through the PAYE system. Partners must also pay income tax on their share of partnership profits. Partnerships only have to account for and pay VAT if they meet the qualifying threshold.

(d) The correct answer is:

	✓
Marketing	✓
Operations	
Human resources	

(e) The correct answer is:

	✓
Human resources	✓
Finance	
Logistics	

(f) The correct answer is:

	✓
Operations	✓
Information technology	
Finance	

The statements are the roles that each of the identified business functions have.

Task 2

(a) The correct answer is:

	✓
The finance director	
The shareholders	
The external auditors	✓
The internal auditors	

(b) The correct answer is:

	✓
The financial accountants	✓
The management accountants	
The Registrar of Companies	
The payroll function	

The external auditors sign an audit report. The accounting records are kept by the financial accountants.

(c) The correct answers are:

	✓
Honest	
Accurate	✓
Available	
Timely	✓
Efficient	
Planned	

The principles of effective communication are complete, accurate, timely and concise.

(d) The correct answers are:

Activity	Solvency ✓	Legal compliance ✓
Monitoring the organisation's cash flow	✓	
Forecasting the organisation's working capital requirements	✓	
Correctly calculating tax liabilities		✓

Monitoring cash flow and forecasting working capital requirements help ensure the organisation can pay its debts when they are due and, therefore, remain solvent.

Paying the correct amount of tax is a legal requirement.

(e)

Task list	Order of task completion
Prepare a report needed by the finance director	First task
Prepare costing calculations needed by the operations director	Second task
Routine tasks	Third task

The report is needed by the finance director by lunchtime so this should be completed first. The costing calculations should be completed next because, although they are not needed until tomorrow, they are more important than your routine tasks and the shredding. The third task will be your routine tasks that you need to do each day. If you have any time left in the afternoon, you could make a start on the shredding.

(f) The correct answer is:

	✓
Refuse to take on the extra work.	
Do the extra work and ignore your routine tasks.	
Speak to your manager about delegating your routine tasks to others while you do the extra work.	✓

 BPP

It would be unprofessional to refuse to do the work or ignore your routine tasks. Speaking to your manager about delegating your routine work while you help with the management accounts is the best solution.

(g) The correct answers are:

Statement	True ✓	False ✓
Accurate information can become inaccurate over time.	✓	
Information is valid if it is appropriate to the use it is being put to.	✓	

Information which is accurate at one time can become inaccurate over time as circumstances change.

Valid information is relevant, strongly associated and appropriate to the use it is being put to.

Task 3

(a) The correct answers are:

Statement	True ✓	False ✓
The objective of CSR policies is to improve the public's perception of the business.		✓
Individuals working within an organisation have a duty to act in accordance with CSR principles.	✓	
Triple bottom line reporting applies only to business activities that affect the environment.		✓

From an organisation's perspective, organisations should truly embody CSR principles rather than adopting them just to improve the public's perception of the business.

Triple bottom line reporting is concerned with business activities and their impact on society and the environment as well as economic impacts.

All individuals working within an organisation have a duty to take responsibility for their actions and to act in a manner consistent with CSR principles.

(b)

Statement	Stakeholder	Internal ✓	External ✓
These stakeholders expect fair and growing remuneration.	Employees	✓	
These stakeholders expect continuity of custom.	Suppliers		✓

Employees are internal stakeholders who expect:

- Fair and growing remuneration
- Career progression
- Safe working environment
- Training

 BPP

- Pension

Suppliers are external stakeholders who expect:

- Fair terms of trade
- Prompt payment
- Continuity of custom

(c) The correct answers are:

	✓
To comply with relevant laws	✓
To act honestly	
To avoid conduct that discredits the profession	✓
To avoid conflicts of interest	

The principle of professional behaviour states that a member shall comply with relevant laws and regulations and avoid any conduct that discredits the profession.

Acting honestly relates to the principle of integrity.

Avoiding conflicts of interest relates to the principle of objectivity.

(d) The correct answers are:

Statement	True ✓	False ✓
If Jenny waits until she has passed a tax exam, she will be deemed competent to perform the calculation.		✓
As this is a private, family matter, professional ethics do not apply.		✓
There is a familiarity threat to Jenny.	✓	

Being professionally competent is more than just passing an exam. It includes experience as well.

Professional ethics apply throughout an accountant's professional and personal life.

Performing a tax calculation for a close relative would create a familiarity threat.

(e) The correct answers are:

	✓
Tell her father she is not professionally competent to perform the calculation.	✓
Refer her father to a tax specialist at work.	✓
Refuse to do the calculation — there is no need to give a reason.	
Perform the calculation but check her calculation afterwards.	

Rather than being silent on the matter and refusing to do the work, Jenny should fulfil the principle of integrity by being open and honest with her father and tell him that she is not professionally competent to perform the calculation. She can refer him to a tax specialist at work who could help instead.

Checking the calculation afterwards still does not mean Jenny was competent to perform the calculation and, in any case, would represent a self-review threat.

Task 4

(a) Purchases day book

Date	Details	Supplier account code	Invoice number	Total	VAT	Net	Product A100	Product B100
20XX				**£**	**£**	**£**	**£**	**£**
30 Jun	GBL Ltd	GBL001	G1161	348	58	290		290
30 Jun	Jackson plc	JAC002	4041	750	125	625	625	
30 Jun	R King	KIN001	J1126	612	102	510	275	235

Purchases returns day book

Date	Details	Supplier account code	Credit note number	Total	VAT	Net	Product A100	Product B100
20XX				**£**	**£**	**£**	**£**	**£**
30 Jun	PDL Designs	PDL001	CN110	912	152	760	560	200
30 Jun	K Ponti	PON002	398C	570	95	475	225	250

(b)

From: Accountingtechnician@XYZ.com

To: Jason@XYZ.com

Cc:

Subject: Purpose of coding systems

Date: 01/10/20XX

Good morning Jason,

Thank you for attending your induction. I hope you are settling in well to your new role.

You may recall at your induction you asked about the purpose of having a coding system for customers and suppliers.

The purpose of having a coding system is to ensure that information, for example invoices and credit notes, are recorded in our accounting system accurately.

Having a unique code for each customer and supplier makes it easy to identify each one. This helps when communicating with them, as well as with the preparation of management reports.

Coding systems also assist with the filing of information. For example, if a customer has a query on their account, we can quickly retrieve any supporting documentation using their unique customer code.

I hope that I have answered your query on the purpose of coding systems, but please let me know if I can clarify anything.

Regards,

(Your name)

Accounting Technician

(c) Any four from the following:

- Increased risk of cyberattacks as the system is online
- Increased risk of loss of, or damage to, data
- Reliance on cybersecurity being provided by the service provider
- Reliance on the service provider maintaining back-ups of company data
- Needing to ensure the cloud accounting subscription is maintained to avoid loss of service
- Queries regarding payment or other account issues may led to services to being withdrawn and data deleted by the service provider
- The need for additional training on cloud accounting
- The need for new guidance and procedures on using cloud-based infrastructures to be created
- New infrastructures may need to be developed to make best use of cloud-based systems

(d)

Gross total	VAT	Net total
£	£	£
277.24	46.21	231.03
163.42	27.24	136.18
49.74	8.29	41.45

VAT = Invoice total × 20/120

Task 5

(a)

Account name	Amount £	Debit ✓	Credit ✓
Suspense	81		✓

Account name	Amount £	Debit ✓	Credit ✓
Suspense	81	✓	

(b)

Account name	Amount £	Debit ✓	Credit ✓
VAT	269		✓

(c)

Account name	Amount £	Debit ✓	Credit ✓
VAT	188	✓	

 BPP

(d) The correct answer is:

	✓
To detect fraud	
To record goods bought on credit	
To record goods sold on credit	
To record non-regular transactions	✓

Task 6

(a) The correct answers are:

Statement	Public law ✓	Private law ✓
A framework of rules provided by Parliament to provide individuals with a system to settle disputes.		✓
Concerns how government and local councils operate but also covers criminal law.	✓	

Private law is a framework of rules provided by Parliament to provide individuals with a system to settle disputes. It is for the individual to take a private law matter to court. Civil law cases come under the private law.

Public law mainly concerns how Government and public organisations (such as councils) operate, but also covers criminal law. Public law cases are brought to court by the state. Criminal law is a type of public law.

(b) The correct answers are:

Statement	Valid offer ✓	Not a valid offer ✓
Goods displayed in a shop window		✓
Public advertisements		✓

Goods displayed in a shop window and public advertisements are examples of invitations to treat and are not valid offers.

(c) The correct answers are:

Statement	Correct ✓	Incorrect ✓
Equitable remedies are awarded if requested by the claimant.		✓
Damages are an equitable remedy.		✓
Damages are generally only payable for economic losses.	✓	

Equitable remedies are awarded at the discretion of the court and are not automatically granted on request by the claimant.

Damages are a common law, not an equitable remedy. They are the usual remedy granted for breach of contract and are used to compensate for economic (financial) losses.

Task 7

(a) Any three from:

- Financial loss
- Damage to reputation
- Loss of faith by customers
- Disruption to the organisation

(b) The correct answer is:

	✓
Relevant and reliable	
Understandable	
Comparable	✓
Timely	

There is a lack of consistency in how the accounts are prepared which means they are not comparable.

(c) The correct answer is:

	✓
Corporate tax payable	
Variance reports	✓
Details of cash balances	
Customer account statements	

Variance reports show how the business is performing against budget. They enable decisions to be made on how to improve performance in the future based on past performance and mistakes.

(d) For the accountant, automation and artificial intelligence (AI) can help in the recording of transactions in financial systems. Accounting software can automatically download transactions from an organisation's online bank account. Once this has been done, the system's IA can assign transactions to appropriate nominal codes and record the transactions appropriately in the accounts. This intelligence is achieved by the user recording the transactions manually a few times before the system learns what types of transactions should be assigned to which nominal codes.

For the auditor, systems are available that perform complete checks on financial data held, allowing 100% of transactions to be audited automatically on a continuous basis, removing the need for an auditor to perform routine audit checks to verify transactions.

Task 8

(a) The correct answer is:

	✓
The company can protect itself from global risk and uncertainty by only trading in its home country.	
The company cannot avoid all risk and uncertainty from the global market.	✓
The company can buy insurance to protect itself from global risks generally.	

Even though the business operates only in its home country, it still operates within the global business environment and will still impacted (to some degree) by global risks and uncertainties (for example the global COVID-19 pandemic impacted most businesses around the world even if they did not trade overseas).

Insurance might be available to protect against specific types of risk (for example, shipping or credit risk). It is not available for global risk generally.

(b) The correct answers are:

Statement	True ✓	False ✓
The equilibrium price is the price of a good where the volume demanded by customers and the volume supplied by businesses are the same.	✓	
Once established, the equilibrium price for a market is fixed.		✓
The equilibrium price is the average price charged for a good in the market.		✓

The equilibrium price is the price of a good where the volume demanded by customers and the volume supplied by businesses are the same. It is not the average price charged for a good.

An equilibrium price is not fixed, but will change as the demand and supply curves shift.

(c) The correct answer is:

	✓
The profit motive describes the purpose of organisations to make their owners wealthier.	✓
All business organisations are motivated by profit.	
Making short-term losses is inconsistent with the profit motive.	

Making the business's owners wealthier is the main motivation for profit-seeking organisations.

Not all businesses are motivated by profit (eg, not-for-profit organisations).

Even though organisations are motivated by making a profit, some might be willing in the short-term to break-even or even make small losses if it means that their market position is strengthened so they can earn larger profits in the future.

(d) The correct answers are:

	Progressive ✓	Regressive ✓	Proportional ✓
The tax rate decreases as the amount to be taxed increases.		✓	
The tax rate increases as the amount to be taxed increases.	✓		
The tax rate is always the same regardless of the level of income.			✓

(e) The correct answer is:

	✓
Transparency	
Certainty	✓
Fairness	

Certainty states that taxes should be clear and easy to understand and calculate.

Transparency aims to prevent individuals and organisations from hiding their affairs and evading tax through global operations.

Fairness states that the right amount of tax should be generated at the right time. The tax system should be designed to prevent instances of double taxation and accidental non-taxation.

(f) The correct answers are:

Statement	Micro-economics ✓	Macro-economics ✓
Relates to a specific industry	✓	
Concerned with issues such as employment levels and inflation		✓
Helps a business decide how much of a product to make	✓	

Micro-economics describes the forces of supply and demand within individual markets (so will help a business decide how much of a product to make). Macro-economics describes the wider economy that all businesses and industries operate in within a particular country.

BPP

(g) The correct answers are:

	✓
Reduce tax but do not reduce government spending	
Increase taxation	✓
Increase government spending but do not alter taxation	
Reduce government spending	✓

Increasing tax and reducing Government spending should reduce the level of aggregate demand. The other policies should increase aggregate demand.

Tell us what you think

Got comments or feedback on this book? Let us know.
Use your QR code reader:

Or, visit:
https://www.smartsurvey.co.uk/s/GPUBYI/

Need to get in touch with customer service?

www.bpp.com/request-support

Spotted an error?

https://learningmedia.bpp.com/pages/errata